and well-dressed to represent any one of the characters mentioned above. Fitted complete in best professional manner as shown at "I" in Fig. 2. Each 15/-
32-inch Knee Figures with 5½-inch heads, and fitted as above described. Each 20/-

Fig. 3.

32-inch Knee Figures with 5½-inch heads, and fitted with *moving glass eyes* and improved mouth movement, handsomely dressed and of superior quality throughout. Each £1 - 7 - 6
38-inch Knee Figures with 6-inch heads, fitted best quality *moving glass eyes* and improved mouth movement, handsomely dressed and of superior quality throughout. Each £1 - 15 - 0
40-inch Knee Figures with 6½-inch heads (small life size) moving glass eyes, moving arm, and all other movements as described above. Very superior. Each £2 - 2 - 0

154.—Special Coster Knee Figure, as used by eminent Music Hall Artistes, 32-inch figure, with 5½-inch head fitted with moving glass eyes, moving arm, &c., &c. Price £1 - 15 - 0
Do. do. 38-inch figure do. ,, £2 - 2 - 0

155.—Box Figures.—This novelty consists of a head in a box, the lid of which opens suddenly, head pops up and talks, interrupting the performer at length, then suddenly disappears into the box. This is repeated as often as desired.
Fitted with best quality 5½-in. heads Price £1 - 1 - 0

156.—Small Standing Figures.—We supply these in any character. They are placed on chairs or table and worked exactly similar to the life-size figures.
32-inch figures with 5½-inch heads, moving glass eyes, and other movements. Price £1 - 15 - 0
Do. do. 38-in. figure, 6¼-in. head ,, £2 - 2 - 0

157.—The "Wonderful Boy" Figure.—This is certainly a most extraordinary figure. In addition to all the ordinary movements the "Wonderful Boy" is constructed to laugh, cry, smoke, wink and move his eyes, flap his ears, knock his hat off, &c.
Life size model Price £3 - 10 - 0

158.—Dancing Nigger.—Arranged on pedestal with handsome back curtain. Legs are worked from behind. The head is thrown back in laughing, the mouth opening very wide. The pedestal forms a box for travelling into which the figure and fittings pack. This figure is very elegantly dressed and is very imposing on the stage. Fitted with all usual movements and finished in best manner throughout. Price £3 - 10 - 0

159.—Laughing Nigger.—This figure stands forty inches high and throws back its head in laughing, the mouth opening very wide. Eyes turn all white; sensation wig, &c. Handsomely dressed as a page.
With mechanical body that enables the nigger to sink down to half his size when the old man attempts to strike him. Great novelty and very laughable. Price £4 - 4 - 0

160.—Small Life Size Sitting Figures.—These are arranged in in a strong packing case and which forms a stand upon which the figure is seated when giving a performance; and with special arrangement for fixing the figure to the stand.
These are usually employed in pairs, and manipulated the one either side of the performer who is seated in a chair; the move-

ments of the *three heads* with the usual argumentative in the extreme. 40 inch figures with moving glass eyes, and all of them handsomely dressed and of a superior quality throughout. Each £3 - 3 - 0
Do. do. full life size do. ,, £4 - 4 - 0

Fig. 4.

161.—Old Man and Old Woman on Chairs.—Handsomely dressed and very superior life size figures. Each in a strong box that forms a chair and which slides with the figures into the box forming a packing case for travelling. The chair backs are turned and ornamented in black and gold. Complete with all movements and actuated in best professional manner as here described and illustrated. The old man may be placed in a variety of grotesque positions; eyes can be made to wink or have the effect of sleeping; sensation wig and arm movements. Kicks the Old Woman, crosses his legs, &c., &c.
The heads of this pair of figures are very carefully modelled and fitted in best manner with moving glass eyes, improved mouth movement, &c. The expression is as near life like as possible.
Per pair £10 - 10 - 0
Carriage of all complete figures to be paid on receipt.

162.—Screen for Stage.—This is about six feet high and very imposing, with massive brass top rail, stand to fix on stage with stage screws, and well trimmed damask curtain. Price £2 - 2 - 0
Carriage to be paid on receipt.

163.—Laughing Heads for Screen.—Nigger, Clown, Quaker, Countryman, &c. Price 20/-, postage 9d.
Head and screen together 55/-
Carriage to be paid on receipt.

Dogs, Cats, Monkeys Birds, Life Size Walking Figures, Life Size Figures on Pedestals, and every conceivable form of mechanical figure made to order.
Extra mechanical movements fitted to any figure, such as smoking arrangement, mechanical hand to take off hat, pneumatic mouth movement, &c., &c. Quotations given free of charge.

BOOKS ON VENTRILOQUISM.

"Practical Ventriloquism" (Ganthony), 155 pages, illustrated.
Price 1/-, postage 3d.
"Hercat's Ventriloquist," 104 pp., Dialogues, &c., Illustrated.
Price 1/-, postage 3d
"Art of Ventriloquism" (Gervaise), 20 Dialogues illustrated.
Price 2/-, postage 3d.
"History of Ventriloquism," (Helm), 42 pages ,, 1/- ,, 2d.
"Maccabe's Ventriloquism," 110 pp., Dialogues, &c.
Price 1/-, postage 2d.

STANYON & CO., Inventors, Manufacturers and Importers of Superior Magical Apparatus,
76, SOLENT ROAD, WEST HAMPSTEAD, LONDON, N.W.

I CAN SEE YOUR LIPS MOVING

THE HISTORY AND ART OF

VENTRILOQUISM

'The Ventriloquist' by Fred Craft, from the cover of 'Country Gentleman' (1922).

I CAN SEE YOUR LIPS MOVING

THE HISTORY AND ART OF VENTRILOQUISM

BY

VALENTINE VOX

PLATO PUBLISHING
North Hollywood, California

in association with

PLAYERS PRESS
Studio City, California
U.S.A.

A.C.T.
AUSTRALIA

Essex
UNITED KINGDOM

Also by Valentine Vox:
Die Geschichte der Bauchrednerkunst
Aerobics Stretch and Shape Workout

Text, photographs and design
by Valentine Vox

Copyright © 1993 by Valentine Vox

All rights reserved. No part of this publication may be reproduced or used in any form or by any means without written permission except in the case of brief quotations embodied in critical articles and reviews.

First published 1981 in Great Britain by Kaye & Ward in association with Plato Publishing (London)

This revised enlarged edition published by Plato Publishing (California), in association with Players Press Inc.

Library of Congress Catalog Number 92-54062
ISBN 0-88734-622-7

Library of Congress Cataloging-in-Publication Data

Vox, Valentine
I can see your lips moving : the history and art of ventriloquism / by Valentine Vox
 p.   cm.
Includes bibliographical references and index.
ISBN 0-88734-622-7 : $34.95
1. Ventriloquism—History. I. Title..
GV1557.V69   1993   92-54062
793.8'9—dc20   CIP

Typeset in the U.S.A. by Unicorn Publishing Services, Los Angeles
Printed in Hong Kong by South China Printing Company

Distributed by Empire Publishing Service
P.O. Box 1344, Studio City, CA 91614-0344
818-784-8918

Contents

Preface		7
Chapter One	Wizards That Peep and Mutter	11
Chapter Two	Diabolical Witchcraft and Ventriloqui	29
Chapter Three	Come and Hear the Change of Voice	41
Chapter Four	From the Sage to the Stage	53
Chapter Five	Vocal Gyrations	71
Chapter Six	Pinocchio Becomes a Boy	87
Chapter Seven	Voices in the Air	113
Chapter Eight	Speaking Dolls	135
Chapter Nine	I Can See Your Lips Moving	165
Chapter Ten	Let Me Out	181
Notes to Chapters		198
Bibliography		207
Acknowledgements		212
Index		214

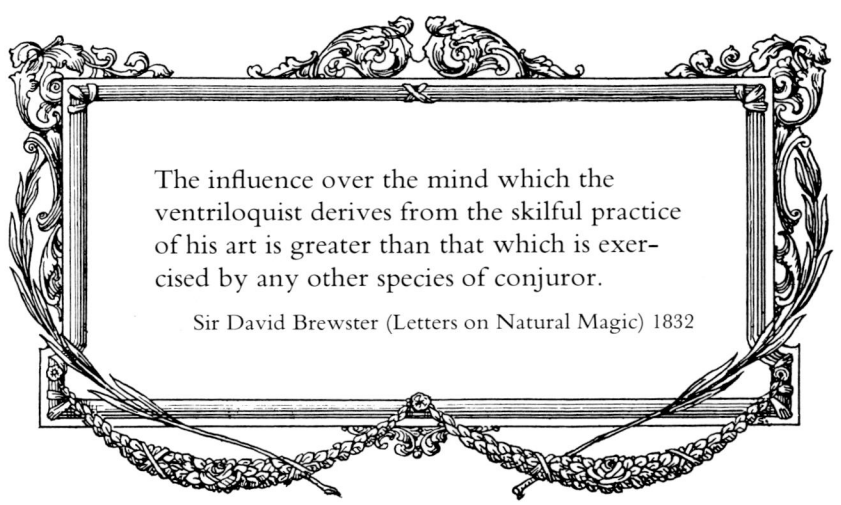

The influence over the mind which the ventriloquist derives from the skilful practice of his art is greater than that which is exercised by any other species of conjuror.

Sir David Brewster (Letters on Natural Magic) 1832

Preface

Ventriloquism is currently enjoyed as an amusing facet of the performing arts but, long before it became an entertainment, it was part of a mystic divining practice, employed by the ancients to call up the spirits of the dead.

The word 'ventriloquist' is derived from the Latin *ventriloquus,* meaning 'belly speaker' rendered from the Greek word 'εγγαστραμυθσς'. Many references are made to ventriloquism in the Bible, and the practice became a debating point among the early Christian fathers who condemned it as a tool of the devil, describing it as an offspring of hell itself.

During the so-called Dark Ages, exponents were regarded as demonic conjurors possessed by unclean spirits that 'lurked in their entrails, from whence they gave their utterances.' The practice of ventriloquism often resulted in imprisonment or death.

In the eighteenth and nineteenth centuries, when ventriloquism emerged as an entertainment, it was still largely misunderstood. Many believed it to be a special talent that enabled certain individuals to throw their voice in any direction.

The facts are otherwise. Ventriloquism is a vocal illusion, defined in most dictionaries as the practice of making the voice appear to come from somewhere other than its source. It can be further explained as the imitation of near and distant sounds. Contrary to popular belief, ventriloquy can be acquired by application and practice. The name is misleading, as ventriloquism does not require any physical abnormality. Ventriloquists do not speak from the stomach, except that they employ the stomach muscles in the same manner as an actor or singer does, to assist the diaphragm to give vocal and tonal strength to the voice.

Ventriloquism takes advantage of the human inability to measure the distance of sound by the ear. Our ears can only judge the distance of sound by previous experience. When we hear a sound, we do not hear the distance from which that sound has travelled; we can only judge by former experiences of hearing similar sounds. Further to this is the association between the ear and the eye. The natural impulse upon hearing a sound is to look and see from where it is proceeding; we automatically use our eyes to pinpoint the source of what we hear. The ventriloquist takes advantage of this fact and will often direct, or rather misdirect, the auditor to the place where he wishes them to hear the sound.

This association between the ear and the eye has been further exploited by the use of the ventriloquial figure, originally known as an automaton or speaking doll. Audiences see the figure's movement and at the same time hear the ventriloquial voice, and their senses are deceived into associating the two. In comparatively recent years, the figure has become the focal point of ventriloquists' performances, and names such as Fred Russell and Coster Joe, Arthur Prince and Jim, Edgar Bergen and Charlie McCarthy were familiar duos associated with the art.

However, before the speaking doll became the fashionable accompaniment for the ventriloquial entertainer, exponents of the art relied solely upon their ability to conjure up sounds that appeared to come from anywhere but themselves. This distant voice ventriloquism, as it is called, is the most skilful aspect of the art, and it has germinated the numerous stories of ventriloquists practicing their skills on their unsuspecting auditors. Over the years these anecdotes have enhanced the mystique surrounding the practice of ventriloquism and, although many stories have no doubt been elaborated upon, they constitute a necessary and colorful part of the history of the ventriloquist's art.

At the turn of the century during the golden age of variety, when the popularity of ventriloquism ensured it a respected place among the performing arts, many ventriloquists enjoyed the sovereignty of topping the bill. Since then, ventriloquism has become a recognized art throughout the world, producing many fine practitioners. Because of the great number of performers, past and present, I am unable to mention everyone. Instead, I have tried to deal with those whose fame or significant contribution to the art warrants their inclusion.

This book is the result of many years of research, and, combined with my own practical knowledge, it presents the first documented study of ventriloquism, from its employment as a divining practice some 3000 years ago to its current application as an entertainment.

Published in the U.S.A. for the first time, fifty pages have been added to this revised, enlarged edition to admit new information, illustrations and a comprehensive bibliography.

I hope that, as well as giving an historical account of ventriloquism, this book will provide the reader with a greater understanding of its development and practice as a performing art.

Valentine Vox
Hollywood
California

DEDICATED TO THE MEMORY OF
EDGAR BERGEN

1

WIZARDS THAT PEEP AND MUTTER

Facing: The ventriloquial figure, commonly known as the dummy or doll, did not become the fashionable accompaniment of the ventriloquist until the latter part of the nineteenth century. This wooden knee figure was employed by Fred Neiman in the eighteen seventies. A simple spring mechanism animates the jaw which is controlled through the back of the head.

'Now you see it, now you don't. The hand is quicker than the eye'. This adage of the eye's vulnerability to deception is familiar to us all. Through their special skills and techniques, magicians take advantage of our visual senses and their tricks and illusions have delighted and baffled observers for thousands of years.

In ancient times, although magic was sometimes enjoyed as a source of amusement, it played a large and important part in many religions. Priests sought keenly after its knowledge believing it to be the faculty whereby they could summon the spirits of their gods. It was a coveted science that, if acquired by man or priest, was thought to be limitless, controlling unseen powers and subordinating them to man's own will. Magic was to the ancient priest what prayer is to the worshipper, an agent of persuasion and communication through which man sought to obtain all things that were not procurable by simple means.[1] It is evident that ancient priests took themselves and their magic very seriously. However, because this magic was mysterious by its very nature, trickery was inevitable and clever charlatans took advantage of the superstitions of ignorant people.

An example of this knavery is reported by the Greek writer Lucian. In AD 150, Alexander of Abonoteichus astonished observers when he displayed a speaking serpent with a human

Below: Fred Nieman with his knee figures (1875).

An artist's reconstruction showing how acoustic tubes were used to make images speak.

head, claiming it to be a god incarnate. Lucian gives a detailed account of how Alexander contrived this so-called miracle: a newly-born snake was placed inside a goose-egg which had previously been blown then resealed with wax. The egg was then buried in some mud at the foundation of a temple. The following morning Alexander pretended to discover it and ran through the streets in a frenzy, making his outrageous claims. Eventually, before a gaping crowd in the market place, he broke open the egg and declared it to be a reincarnated god.[2]

Once the secret of any trick or illusion is known, the mystery is gone and it becomes almost laughable. Lucian's explanation certainly had this result, but the secret was not known to those who witnessed Alexander's display of 'magic'. They believed what they saw and accepted it as a miracle.

Apart from the eye, the ear is the most easily deceived organ; Alexander of Abonoteichus did not overlook this fact either. After caring for the reptile for many months, he displayed the serpent fully grown, bearing a human head which spoke and gave oracular advice on every subject.

Lucian's account explained that the head was constructed from linen and the mouth was made to move by means of horse-hairs. The vocal effect was achieved by a tube fastened inside the head which led in turn to a concealed assistant who, by speaking into the tube, gave the impression that the serpent was talking. Lucian called the tube an 'autophone'.[3]

Although Alexander's speaking serpent was certainly ingenious, its vocal mechanics were by no means new. Archaeologists have since unearthed similar apparatus used by the ancients. In the ruins near Alba, Italy, pipelines were discovered leading to hidden chambers in which priests could hide undetected and, by speaking into the various conduits, could make their voices heard in almost every part of the sanctuary.[4] During the first century A.D., it is not difficult to imagine that the mystic philosopher Apollonius took advantage of a similar arrangement when a tree was heard uttering words in his presence in a 'clear voice resembling a woman'.[5]

A more recent version of this ancient deception was found a little over a hundred years ago in China where, in an obscure village, the secrets of a talking idol were exposed. The image stood on a platform inside a shrine, and local peasants reported that it spoke at certain times. Worshippers who were present during these rare occasions deemed themselves recipients of high favour and great blessing. Upon close examination, it was found that a tube passed from the head of the figure to a wall directly

The Memnon Colossi, the only remains of the funerary temple of King Amenophis III at Thebes. The northern Colossus (right) is the famous speaking Memnon which, on certain days at sunrise, emitted a musical sound.

Facing: 'The Two Diviners' by J.L. Gerome, inspired by the famous saying by Cato, who wondered how two diviners could meet without laughing.

behind it. When anybody spoke into the tube the sound of the voice emanated from the head, the hollowness of which gave the voice a deep, cavernous tone.[6]

In ancient times, many natural sounds such as the rush of water or the roll of thunder were often interpreted as supernatural vocal transmissions. During the Graeco-Roman period, thousands of people left graffiti testimony upon 'hearing' the Egyptian statue of Memnon 'speak'.[7] This phenomenon of musical sound has since been attributed to the sudden expansion of stone caused by the early morning sunlight, although the ancients believed it to be the voice of the gods.

Today, thanks to modern communications, the transmission of the voice is an everyday occurrence. But in ancient times, when man groped his way through entangling superstitions and fear of the unknown, it is not difficult to imagine how the natural phenomena of sound transmission and crude acoustic methods were enough to be labelled miraculous.

Magic was one of the two major elements in the study of the occult. The other was divination–the foretelling of future or hidden things by various means. A magician was not primarily concerned with foretelling the future or preventing something from happening in the normal course of events. He would perform a trick to achieve a particular result, perhaps appearing to decapitate a body and make it whole again, or to change a rod into a serpent. On the other hand, a diviner would observe certain signs and omens through which he would endeavour to reveal the future or secret things.[8]

Born out of man's natural desire to know the future, the variety of divinatory methods was immense. Diviners studied the movements of water (hydromancy), the entrails of beasts (haruspicy) and the flights of birds (ornithomancy). Halomancy was the use of salt in divination, anthroposcopy the study of the facial features and cheiromancy was the study of the hands.

Although incomplete, this list gives an idea of the vast area covered by divinatory practices. Scarcely an object moved in the heavens or on the earth without being used to interpret a message of futurity. Sometimes the most trivial occurrences, such as sneezing or coughing (cledonomancy), were invested with meaning, prompting the Roman Cato to wonder how two diviners could possibly meet without laughing.[9] Many of these ancient studies are still practised today, particularly astrology and palmistry, the latter surviving in almost its original form.

Another study that has endured is necromancy or divination by communication with the dead. The belief that death increases

Priests or necromancers evoking the dead (Gems). Fifth Century B.C.

Facing: The witch of Endor calling up the voice of the prophet Samuel. This act by the witch caused much of the controversy among the early Christian fathers concerning ventriloquism.
Above the head of the witch is the mysterious Hebrew word Obh, which the Septuagint translates as ventriloquist. The word, which occurs several times in the bible, also means a bottle or something hollow. A similar word appears in the Arabic وأبة *(Wa-ba), meaning a hole in a rock or pit.*
Although the etymology is uncertain, the most common derivation is attributed to the hollow cavernous sounds made by the necromancer to simulate the departed spirits.[17]
(Drawing by Raffaele Pellizzari)

rather than diminishes a man's powers, especially his prophetic faculties, is the basis of necromancy. The ancient necromancer would evoke or claim to possess the spirit of the dead within him, and through the dead be able to reveal and foretell the future. It is from the practice of necromancy that ventriloquism finds its origin.[10]

In the Mosaic law given to the Israelites about 1500 BC, necromancy and occult practices were strictly forbidden. In Deuteronomy 18:9 (Authorized Version), we read, 'When thou art come to the land which the Lord thy God giveth thee, thou shalt not learn to do after the abominations of those nations. There shall not be found among you anyone that maketh his son or daughter pass through fire, or that useth divination, or an observer of times, or an enchanter or a witch, or a charmer, or a consulter with familiar spirits, or a wizard, or a necromancer. For all these things are an abomination to the Lord.'[11]

Divining by a 'familiar spirit' was a form of necromancy called in the original Hebrew 'Obh' (אוֹב) denoting the soothsaying spirit of the dead.[12] To evoke 'Obh', the necromancer would stoop down and feign a hollow voice that seemed to come from the lower joints or the ground.[13] The enquirer was led to believe that this was the voice of the spirit of 'Obh'. Isaiah 29:4 indicates explicitly the manner of speech used by those who evoke the spirit of 'Obh'.[14]

'. . and thou shalt be brought down and shall speak out of the ground, and thy speech shall be made low out of the dust, and thy voice shall be as one who hath a familiar spirit (Obh) out of the ground, and thy speech shall whisper out of the dust'.

In conjunction with this, Isaiah 8:19 mentions the 'wizards that peep and mutter'.[15]

Although it carried the death penalty, necromancy was still practiced in Israel. The first book of Samuel (I. Sam. 28) relates the classic story of the meeting between King Saul and the female necromancer at Endor. Saul, threatened by the Philistine armies and finding his prayers unanswered, turned in desperation to necromancy and bade his servants find him a person 'who hath a familiar spirit' or, literally, 'one who is a possessor of Obh'. Obeying his command, his servants escorted the dispirited king to a small hamlet just south of Mount Tabor, where Saul persuaded a witch, described in the original Hebrew as 'Baalat-Obh' (בַּעֲלַת אוֹב) 'the possessor of Obh', to call forth the spirit of the deceased prophet Samuel.[16]

During the evocation, the woman suddenly discovered that the enquirer was Saul, the king, and refused to continue for fear

Bust of Hippocrates, the Greek father of Medicine, who was one of the earliest writers to mention ventriloquism in his work on Epidemics.

of her life. But Saul assured her that no harm would come to her and commanded her to continue with the seance. The witch then claimed to see an old man coming up out of the ground, and Saul, 'perceiving it was Samuel', fell to the ground, whereupon the apparition was heard to speak, predicting forthcoming doom.[18]

Saul's weak physical condition and his desperation to obtain an answer left doubt as to whether the voice he heard was in fact that of the prophet Samuel or whether it was a cunning trick performed by the witch through the acquired skill of ventriloquy. This latter view is strongly supported by the context; it is not clear that Saul actually saw the ghost at all. Also the apparition's responses consisted mainly of oracular echoes to Saul's questions.

In the Greek version of the scriptures (Septuagint), translated by Hebrew scholars in the third century BC, the words 'Baal Obh', the necromancer, are rendered as $\epsilon\gamma\gamma\alpha\sigma\tau\rho\alpha\mu\nu\theta\sigma\varsigma$, meaning 'ventriloquist', compounded of $\epsilon\gamma$ ('in') $\gamma\alpha\sigma\tau\rho$ ('belly') and $\mu\nu\theta\sigma\varsigma$ ('speaker').[19]

Belly speakers, or belly prophets, as they were sometimes called, would counterfeit spirit possession by talking in a diffused voice while engaging in a certain amount of lip control. The enquirer was led to believe that the voices heard came from the diviner's stomach where the departed spirit was thought to dwell. In Greece this mode of divination was called gastromancy ($\gamma\alpha\sigma\tau\rho\sigma\mu\alpha\nu\tau\epsilon\nu\epsilon\sigma\theta\alpha\iota$).[20]

In his fifth book on epidemics, the Greek doctor and philosopher Hippocrates gives an example of the delusive voice employed by those practicing gastromancy. Describing the symptoms of a patient whose voice had become weak and faint, he said, 'The sound seemed to come from the chest, similar to that uttered by the so-called ventriloquists',[21] a description that corresponds with the low whispering voice described in Isaiah 29:4.

The feigned voice could either articulate words or give convulsive moans and utterances, depending on the skill of the diviner. In the fifth century BC, one of the most skilful exponents of this practice was an Athenian priest named Eurycles. Plato called him 'the strange Eurycles',[22] and his notoriety was such that an entire school of ventriloquizing prophets was named after him (Eurycleis). At the time, his counterpart in Egypt was Sacchura, who was called 'wizard of the dead'.[23]

Not everyone took Eurycles' vocal jugglery seriously at the time. Aristophanes, the Greek playwright, comically compared himself with the priest and, in so doing, coined the time honoured pun of ventriloquism. 'He wrote, 'he was ever your savior from

Haruspicy: A bronze mirror-back shows a Greek diviner examining the liver of a sacrificed animal. Fourth Century B.C.

Below: Cheiromancy. A Roman soldier seeks to learn his future from the reading of his palm.

his first incognito essays at the stage when he took a leaf from the book of that sage ventriloquist-prophet Eurycles and cast his voice into others' mouths'.²⁴

In this play, *Wasps,* first produced in 422 BC, Aristophanes implied that Eurycles' voice diffusion was so well-managed that it appeared to come from another source and that he himself, in the same manner, wrote words to put into the mouths of actors.

Eurycles and the many other seers and soothsaying prophets who lived in the fifth century BC, sometimes peddled their revelations from house to house. There were also special temples, built to pronounce the oracles of the gods. The most famous of these ancient shrines was at Delphi, on Mt. Parnassus. The innermost sanctuary of this temple was where the gods' oracles were revealed through a priestess called Pythia, who was named after a serpent that the god Apollo had killed.²⁵

The ancient Pythia seated in the temple of Apollo where priests anxiously wait to interpret her utterances.

In a state of self-induced frenzy, the priestess would give voice to the gods' revelations. Her ambiguous utterances, which were sometimes no more than incoherent groans, were quickly interpreted by waiting priests, and in their turn, poets put them into verse. Although Pythia's prophetic mode differed from that of Eurycles, who appeared to be fairly articulate and who apparently needed no interpreter, her changes of voice and convulsive groans were characteristic of the ventriloquial practice employed to counterfeit spirit possession. In his *De Oraculo Defecto* written in the first century A.D., Plutarch uses the word ventriloquist (ἐγγαστραμυθὸς) to describe the style both of the Pythones and the Eurycleis, and wrote, 'Certainly it is foolish and childish in the extreme to imagine that the god himself after the manner of ventriloquists, who used to be called 'Eurycleis' but now 'Pythones', enters into the bodies of his prophets and prompts their utterances, employing their mouths and voices as instruments'.[26]

As Plutarch stated, the ventriloquistic diviners in the first century A.D. gradually became known as 'Pythones' instead of Eurycleis. Sophocles added another description, calling them 'Sternomantics' (στερνομαντις), or those who prophesy from the chest.[27]

There seems little doubt that whether they were called Eurycleis, Pythones or Sternomantics, ventriloquistic diviners in ancient Greece were among the most prominent foretellers of the future.

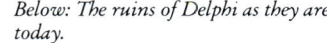

Below: The ruins of Delphi as they are today.

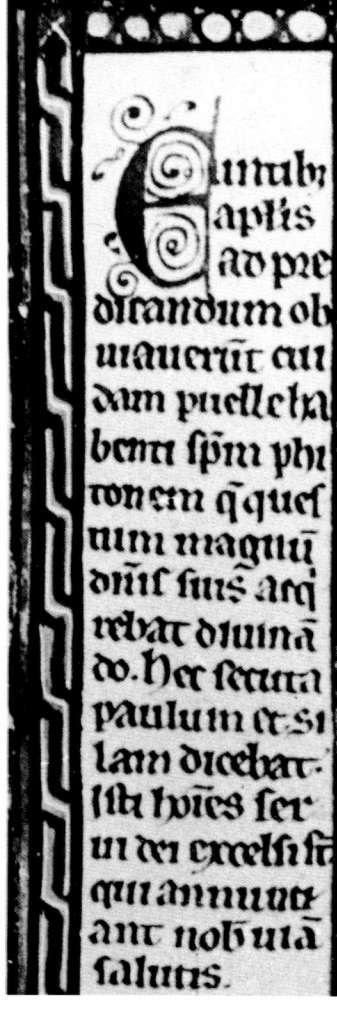

Above: The girl with the familiar spirit mentioned in the Acts of the Apostles. St. Augustine referred to her as a female ventriloquist.

Although it might have been used for dishonest gain, their unusual faculty of vocal evocation earned them the awe, if not the respect, of their contemporaries.

During the Graeco-Roman period, the influence of the oracles began to decline, though the one at Delphi continued to be consulted. The Etruscans, as well as the Greeks, exerted a strong influence on the Roman religion, which was a composite of many elements derived from the numerous cultures with which Rome came in contact.[28]

In the reign of Augustus Caesar there emerged a new religion which, despite the execution of its leader and the persecution of his followers, grew with amazing rapidity. This new creed, Christianity, showed no tolerance towards the many religious and divinatory practices of the day, and claimed that the sole hope of salvation lay in Jesus Christ. In spite of this 'good news', the practice of divination continued to thrive. In the sixteenth chapter of the Acts of the Apostles, Luke related the story of the slave girl who had a 'familiar spirit', which he calls, in the original Greek Πνθωνας (Pythones).²⁹ St. Augustine refers to this same girl as a *femina ventriloqua*,³⁰ and in later writings, 'Pythones' often appear synonymous with the Latin noun *ventriloquus*. This word, which has survived in almost its original form, is the Latin rendering of the Greek, compounded of *venter* and *loquor* ('belly' and 'to speak').

In the second century AD, Tertullian, quoting Isaiah in his work *Adversus Marcionem*, wrote, *Quis alius disiciet signa ventriloquorum et divinationes ex corde, avertens in posterioria sapientes et cogitationes eorum infatuans?* ('Who else shall frustrate the signs of the ventriloquists and their divinations out of their heart, turning wise men backward and making their cogitations foolish?')³¹

It appears that the ventriloquistic diviners were not only popular during Roman times but gained as much prominence as the more notable forms of divination. St. Clement wrote 'The ventriloquists are still held in honor by many', and he placed them beside the Augurs and the Pythia.³²

Not all the early Christian fathers accepted the delusive ability of the ventriloquistic diviners. In the third century, Origen, writing his commentary on the book of Samuel, did not support the view that the voice of the prophet was raised by the witch of

The witch of Endor raising the ghost of Samuel (19th century print). The belief that the ghost of Samuel actually appeared and spoke during this seance was the view held by Origin in his homily written in the third century that began a controversy on ventriloquism.

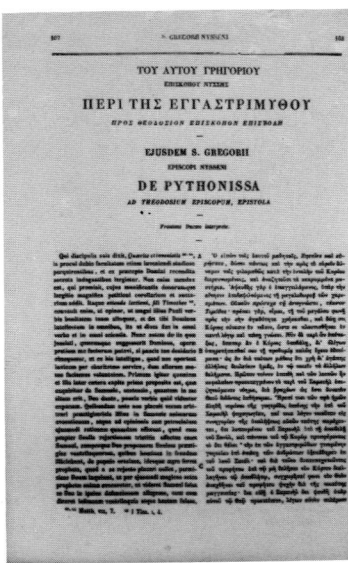

'The Ventriloquist', the treatise written by St. Gregory in the fourth century concerning the controversy about the witch of Endor.

Endor ventriloquially, contending that the ghost of Samuel really appeared and spoke with Saul.[33]

Disputing this view, two ecclesiastics, St. Gregory and Eustathius, wrote special treaties on ventriloquism in answer to Origen's. In his short work entitled *De Pythones*, St. Gregory argued that God would not have allowed Samuel's ghost to be conjured up by a practice that He had forbidden, and also said that Samuel's spirit was already in paradise and could not therefore be disturbed.[34] Eustathius supported this view in his treatise, *The Ventriloquist, contrary to Origen*, and furthermore, likened the whole episode to the same kind of trickery that had been exercised by Pharoah's magicians at the time of Moses when they changed their rods into serpents. Eustathius also contended that the predictions made by the feigned ghost were inaccurate, therefore not divinely inspired.[35]

Although these writers argued whether or not the whole episode had depended on trickery, all agreed on one point: ventriloquism was not merely a vocal deception, but rather ventriloquistic diviners were possessed by demons. This view, which affirmed that the practice of ventriloquism was supernatural, continued throughout early Christian teaching. Warning young Christians on the downfall of gluttony, St. Clement wrote, 'Those who bend around inflammatory tables, nourishing their own diseases, are ruled by a most lickerish demon whom I shall not blush to call the Belly-demon, and he is the worst and most abandoned of all demons. He is therefore exactly like the one who is called a Ventriloquist-demon'.[36]

Another second century writer who employed a similar allegory was Lucian in his work *Lexiphanes*. However, in his usual manner of scorning the superstitions of the day, Lucian found the practice a source of amusement. After Lexiphanes had swallowed some medicine which caused his stomach to rumble, he said, 'What is this? I seem to have swallowed a ventriloquist!'.[37]

There was a period in human thought when the whole universe seemed to be motivated by the spiritual world, but today, in the light of increased knowledge and understanding, new causes have been assigned to the operations of nature and the events of life. No more is the simmering volcano seen as a spiritual manifestation or the roll of thunder as the angry voice of the gods; instead, these natural phenomena are understood and accepted as part of the vast cosmos which surrounds us.

Although many practices of ancient societies are occasionally revived–for example witchcraft–much that the ancients took seriously has become the sport of later generations. This is

A female medium conducts a seance (19th century print). In the Orient a small doll was sometimes employed by ventriloquial diviners. The responses heard seemed to come from the figure.

particularly true of ventriloquism and its kindred practice, magic. In modern society, the magician is not a mediator for good or evil, nor is the ventriloquist seen as a demonic conjuror. Instead, both are seen as artists providing enjoyment and entertainment.

However, in many cultures throughout the world, magic and divination are still employed as they were thousands of years ago, and it is not surprising to find ventriloquism used as it was in the past. In Guinea, for instance, the fetish-woman crouches to the ground, her head between her legs and her hands clasped to her face, while her consulter inquires of her 'familiar'. The questions asked could concern a matter of life and death– whether a family member will die of a disease that has suddenly seized him or her– or be quite a trivial domestic matter such as the whereabouts of a lost object. The ambiguous replies that appear to come from the ground are heard in 'a thin, whistling voice'. The answers delivered by the medium may include the killing of a white cock as a sacrifice to redeem the lost object, or the driving of some wooden pegs into the ground–thus burying the disease.[38]

To evoke their 'familiar', diviners sometimes work themselves into a state of self-induced frenzy, reminiscent of the ancient Pythia. The Fijian priest stares in silence at a whale's tooth, then suddenly twitches and trembles, gradually working himself into strong convulsions until, 'with a change of voice', he finally gives the divine answer.[39]

In many rural areas of the Orient, it has been found that female mediums sometimes employ a tiny doll, and the responses appear to come from the figure, which the diviner rests on her stomach.[40] The ventriloquistic diviner is also found among the primitive peoples of Africa. There the Zulu witchdoctor may be visited by his 'familiar', Amatogo. 'The voice', said a native witness, 'was like that of a little child speaking from the wattles of the hut'.[41]

In the northern Polar regions, the primitive ventriloquist was graphically described by Captain Edward Lyon during his explorations in the 1820s. He wrote:[42]

'All lights excluded, our sorcerer began chanting to his wife with great vehemence and she, in turn, began answering by singing the Amma-aya, which was not discontinued during the whole ceremony. As far as I could hear he afterwards began turning himself rapidly around and, in a loud and powerful voice, vociferated for 'Tornga' with great impatience, at the same time blowing and snorting like a walrus. His noise, impatient and agitated, increased every moment, and he at length seated himself on the floor, varying his tones and making a rustling noise with his clothes. Suddenly, the voice seemed smothered and so well managed as to sound as if retreating beneath the floor, each moment becoming more distant, and ultimately giving the idea of being many feet below the cabin, where it ceased entirely. His wife, now, in answer to queries, informed me very seriously that he had dived, and that he would send up Tornga. Accordingly, in about a half a minute a distant blowing was heard, slowly, very slowly approaching, and a voice which differed from that which we at first heard was at times mingled with blowing until, at length, both sounds became distinct and the old woman informed me that Tornga was coming up to answer my questions.

I, accordingly, asked several questions of the sagacious spirit, to each of which my enquirer received an answer by two loud slaps on the floor which I was given to understand as favourable. A very hollow yet powerful voice, certainly much different from the tones of Toolmak, now chanted for some time, and a strange jumble of hisses, groans,

Below: The African Witchdoctor.

and shouts and gabblings like a turkey succeeded in rapid order. The old woman sang with increased energy and, as I took it for granted that this was all intended to astonish the Kabloona, I cried repeatedly that I was much afraid. This, as I expected, added fuel to the fire, until the poor mortal, exhausted by his own might, asked leave to retire. The voice gradually sank from our hearing as at first, and a very distinct hissing sound succeeded. In its advance it sounded like the tone produced by the wind on the base cord of an Eolian harp. This was soon changed to a rapid hiss like that of a rocket, and Toolmak with a loud yell announced his return. I had held my breath at the first distant hissing and twice exhausted myself, yet our conjuror did not once respire, and his returning and powerful yell was uttered without a previous stop or inspiration of air. Light being admitted, our wizard, as might be expected, was in profuse perspiration, and certainly much exhausted by his exertions, which had continued for at least half an hour.'

By observing the primitive employment of this present-day art, we hold a mirror to the past and understand more fully how ancients like Eurycles used the unusual skill of ventriloquism. At the same time, it is sometimes difficult to grasp the fact that practices which have become sport in modern society still play an important part in primitive religion where they continue to be employed as they were thousands of years ago.

Eskimo Shaman (19th century print). Below: An Eskimo Shaman seeks to cure a headache.

2

Facing: A group of figures made by Len Insull from 1930 to 1950 (composite). All have a leather mouth movement and either balanced or manually-operated eyes. In addition, some of these figures move their ears, smile and wink each eye independently.

DIABOLICAL WITCHCRAFT AND VENTRILOQUI

Throughout the Middle Ages, ventriloquism remained a topic of discussion in theological debates and treatises, largely with regard to the witch of Endor.

In 850 AD Photius, the patriarch of Constantinople, wrote, 'It is a wickedness lurking in the human belly and deserving to dwell in the cesspool, an impure breath which some people, on account of their overwhelming pity, call ventriloquism'.[1] The staunch position by the church associating ventriloquism with witchcraft and demonology undoubtedly caused its suppression, and it is not without reason that we find little mention of ventriloquism being practiced during this period.

When Constantine embraced the church in 470 AD, divination and occult practices were forbidden.[2] This suppression continued, growing fiercer, until in the thirteenth century, a spirit of religious persecution towards paganism caused the inhumane practice of witchhunting. People who were crippled or deformed with age could be worth twenty shillings to a witchfinder, for individuals caught exercising any kind of unusual practice, whether for their own amusement or not, were often sentenced to death.

Thousands of people suffered during those dreadful days between the thirteenth and the seventeenth centuries and ven-

Below: The author at age 12, performing with an Insull figure.

Henry VIII and Anne Boleyn.

Facing: Elizabeth Barton, the Holy Maid of Kent, whose ventriloquial utterances against the marriage of Henry VIII and Anne Boleyn resulted in her execution.

triloquism is often mentioned as being part of the magical practice of witchcraft. In 1370, Nichol Oreseme, the Bishop of Lisieux stated that ventriloquism was the third base of the magical practice. Oreseme divided the magical arts into three roots, 'false persuasion', 'the application of things' and 'the power of words'. In the latter he explained how 'sounds have great and wonderful efficacies and the sound most endowed with this power is the human voice' which magicians use to derange men's minds. Ventriloquism, he said, was the 'difformity of the voice which the magician emits from the depth of his breast, and then it is thought that the demon is speaking in him or under the earth.'[3]

The Reformation brought little relief from the persecution of so-called witches throughout Europe; Protestants were as guilty as Catholics of this inhumane practice, carried out in the name of religion. Prior to the marriage of Henry VIII to Anne Boleyn, which finalized the inevitable split with Rome, the ventriloquial utterances of a young woman in Kent tried to prevent this Royal union.

Elizabeth Barton, commonly known as the 'Holy Maid of Kent' was described in the sixteenth century as a *ventriloqua*, as she spoke with a 'voice from within her belly'. Many believed that she was divinely inspired and thousands of pilgrims flocked to Adlington to hear her oracular utterances. She first experienced her clairvoyancy at nineteen while employed as a servant in the household of Thomas Cobb, and she later became a nun. Her oracles were delivered in a trance-like state, when she spoke 'sweetly and heavenly' of the joys of paradise and 'horribly and terribly' of the torments of hell.[4]

Her ventriloquial utterances were described by the Archbishop of Canterbury Thomas Cranmer in 1533, and he wrote, 'There was a voice speaking from within her belly, as though it were a tun, her lips not greatly moving'.[5] Whether these 'oracles' were divinely inspired or feigned by ventriloquial trickery was as much a debating point among Christians as had been the powers of the witch of Endor among early scholars.

The maid's prophecies opposing Henry's marriage to Anne Boleyn eventually led to her arrest. She was tried and found guilty of high treason. In her confession at the scaffold, she admitted that her prophetic utterances had been fraudulent, contrived by men of learning for their own gain. She was hanged at Tyburn on April 20, 1534.

By the latter half of the sixteenth century, a more rational spirit was abroad. Men were developing new thoughts and ideas

about the world. Tremendous advances were made in science and technology, and the invention of movable type accelerated the exchange of thoughts and information. A new-found interest in scientific inquiry caused many people to question their age-old beliefs about witchcraft.

In 1584 Reginald Scot published his voluminous work, *The Discoverie of Witchcraft*. This rejected the prevailing belief that witchcraft and magic were supernatural practices, and explained the ways in which many sleight-of-hand tricks and illusions were performed. The book devoted a whole chapter to ventriloquism and, although Scot did not explain how it was done, he did expose it as trickery, saying, 'The Pythones spake hollow as in the bottom of their bellies, whereby they are aptly called *ventriloqui*. These are such as take upon themselves to give oracles, to tell where things lost are become and finally to appeach others of mischief, which they themselves most commonly have brought to pass'.[6]

Scot also quoted the testimony of a self-confessed *ventriloqua*,

Below: The hanging of witches in the seventeenth century. On the right of the picture a witch finder receives payment for the discovery of a coven.

Mildred Norrington, who practiced her 'diabolical witchcraft and *ventriloqui*' at Westwell in 1574, characterizing the Holy Maid of Kent.[7] Not only did Scot attempt to deride belief in witchcraft, but he also tried to cause the cruel practice of witch-hunting to fall into disrepute.

In spite of Scots exposé and the changes taking place in the civilized world, the witchhunting mania continued, and having a 'familiar' (familiar spirit) was one of the prime accusations against those tried for witchcraft. It was believed that witches had familiars or imps in constant attendance, often disguised as different creatures. The term 'familiar' was exclusively English, taken from the Authorized Version of the Bible and the story of the witch of Endor. In 1645 during the witch trials conducted by

The frontispiece to Matthew Hopkins' 'Discovery of Witches' (1647).

King James I, who believed in witchcraft and advocated the persecution of witches. He called Reginald Scot's book 'damnable' and ordered all copies to be burnt.[10]

Matthew Hopkins, the notorious witchfinder General, he testified, under oath, that he had both seen and heard the familiars of those accused, that he said resembled various animals.[8]

In the trial of Elizabeth Clark, Hopkins named the familiars he had proported to have witnessed. 'Holt a white kitten, Jamara a fat spaniel, Vinegar Tom a long-legged greyhound, Sack and Sugar a black rabbit and News a polecat.' Hopkins claimed to have seen these imps in Elizabeth Clark's cell before she was tried and hanged along with six other women accused of witchcraft.

During his reign of terror, Hopkins was responsible for the hanging of at least two hundred persons, most of whom were executed on no other account but that of harboring familiar spirits.[9]

The Church held fast to many of its beliefs and ventriloquism continued to be regarded as a practice spawned by hell itself. Christian writers at the time took great pains to make it look as evil as possible. Augustine Eugubinus wrote, 'We have seen women in our own times sitting down and uttering words from their genitals. The Greek fathers tell us of one such woman who is supposed to be the Pythia, whose extremely unclean devil chose the vagina and anus part of the body to dwell'.[11] The lower parts of the body were seen by many as a suitable habitation for this 'most unclean devil'. Some suggested that 'evil spirits lurked in their entrails from whence they gave their utterances'.[12] Despite this stigma, the sixteenth century was a significant turning point of this practice that had so far been attributed to witchcraft.

In 1550 Jean Brodeau related the story of Louis Brabant, who managed to obtain a wife and a considerable amount of money through his ventriloquial abilities.[13] Brabant, who was *valet de chambre* to Francis I, had fallen in love with a beautiful young heiress but, because of Brabant's humble position, the girl's father refused to allow them to marry. Undaunted, Brabant continued to woo the young maid, and when her father suddenly died he asked for her mother's consent to the marriage but, respecting her late husband's wishes, she refused. Brabant then asked the mother if he could arrange a seance to contact her husband's spirit in a final attempt to convince the deceased of his worthiness. It was during this seance that Brabant cunningly employed his ventriloquial talents. In a voice that appeared to come from some distance, he called the mother by name, claiming to be the deceased father, now in Purgatory. The voice bade the mother grant her consent to the marriage and, in doing so, relieve the father's torment, 'as Brabant was a fine person and

Reginald Scot's 'Discoverie of Witchcraft', published in 1584. The author devoted a chapter to ventriloquism, rejecting it as supernatural and exposing it as a form of conjuring.

refusal would be unjust'. The mother was convinced that she heard her late husband's voice and immediately gave the couple her blessing.

Brabant had another obstacle to overcome– his lack of money. Deciding to employ his ventriloquy further, he arranged a meeting with a Monsieur Comu, a miser from Lyons, and once more used his ventriloquial skill. This time the distant voice that Brabant assumed was that of Comu's father, who apparently insisted that he give Brabant a large sum of money to be used to purchase Christian freedom from the Turks. But the old miser did not comply, and Brabant had to arrange another meeting, this time at Comu's request, in an open field. The ventriloquial demands were repeated just as effectively; Comu parted with his money and Brabant took his bride.[14]

This story, which amused Francis I, was no doubt exaggerated but, nevertheless, its fabrication does possess an element of truth. In all probability, Brabant did have extraordinary vocal ability with which he often entertained his fellow workers and the king himself. What is of particular interest in this colorful sixteenth century story is that, for the first time, the ventriloquist was no longer a demon-possessed warlock from hell, but rather a romantic rogue who engaged his unusual talent to win the woman he loved.

The French continued to show tolerance towards exponents of *ventriloque* and allowed themselves to be amused by its practice. In 1624, the powerful and influential Cardinal Richelieu engaged a ventriloquist to frighten one of his bishops. The ventriloquist, Monsieur Collet, was named 'the spirit of Montemare', because the voice he assumed appeared to come from above. The cardinal had arranged for the ventriloquist to hide himself in the midst of a procession that followed him to the Tuileries. Among this crowd was Bishop Raconis, on whom the joke was to be played. After they had walked a short way a voice was heard calling, 'Abra de Raconis, Abra de Raconis'. The bishop turned around, but saw nothing. The voice continued calling until Raconis, trembling with fear, ran forward and addressed the cardinal saying, 'Monseigneur, I ask your forgiveness if I am losing respect of your Grace, but I can hear a voice calling me from the air'. The cardinal and the other ecclesiastics, who were aware of the hoax, insisted that they heard nothing. Then the cardinal asked for silence and the voice called Raconis again, this time warning him against 'seeking favour with high society'. Raconis, thinking that the devil himself was after him, went as pale as a ghost and had to be taken to his home where it took some time to convince him that it was all a joke.[15]

In England, ventriloquism was gradually emerging as an amusement, and in 1655 a man called 'Fannigus' delighted the English court with his remarkable ventriloquial skill.[16]

Known as 'The king's whisperer', he was noted for his ability of 'uttering whatsoever he wished without moving his lips, so that the words seemed to come from some distance'. On one occasion, the king summoned a knight to his private chambers on the pretext of having a serious consultation. The ventriloquist stood nearby and, as the knight bent his ear to the king's attention, a voice was heard calling him, 'Sir John, Sir John, come away'. When the voice persisted the knight begged leave of the king, and went into the other room 'to find whoever it was that dare call him from the king's presence'. Finding nobody, he returned to the king. The voice was then heard calling him again, and this time it 'caused the knight to stamp with madness'. Finally, after the king had enjoyed himself sufficiently at the knight's expense, he confessed to the hoax.[17]

In 1661, Leo Allatius compiled two comprehensive treatises on ventriloquism, *De Engastrimthyo Syntagma* and *De*

Below: *An audience with Cardinal Richelieu from the painting by Adrien Moreau. Cardinal Richelieu once employed a ventriloquist to frighten one of his bishops.*

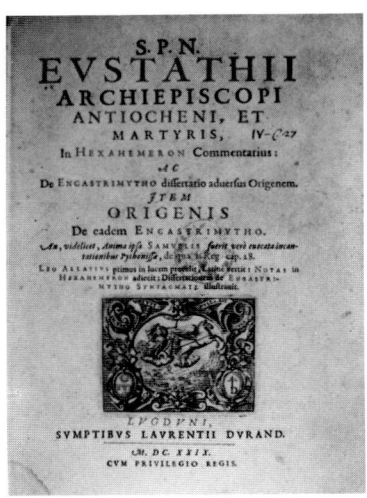

Leone Allatius's comprehensive treatise on ventriloquism, written in 1661 when Allatius was the Vatican librarian.

Engastrimytho Dissertatio.[18] Allatius was the Vatican librarian and responsible for bringing to light the ventriloquial tract on the witch of Endor by Eustathius, which he found in an old manuscript. Together with other works on the subject, Allatius compiled a detailed study of ventriloquism. While his introduction is of particular interest, being 'a collection of references on ventriloquism', he nevertheless dealt with the old theological controversies and affirmed the standpoint of the Church in regarding the practice as Satanic.

As the seventeenth century drew to a close, ventriloquism was either viewed as demonic possession or a deception acquired through practice. 'Could there be ventriloquists without the aid of the devil?' was the question posed by one writer of the time.[19] This uncertainty was further indicated in Blount's dictionary (1688), 'Ventriloquist: One who hath an evil spirit speaking from his belly or, one that can by use and practice speak as it were out of his belly'.[20]

This division is significant; on one hand, ventriloquism is seen as a harmless acquired practice, while, on the other, it is regarded as demonic possession.

Scientific opinions also differed. Julius Casserius, an Italian anatomist, maintained that ventriloquism could only be explained as a magical power. In his *Anatomical History of the Voice and Hearing Organs* (1601) he wrote, 'We have been told and we have read that few people have the ability of making a very well articulated voice heard from within the belly and the chest, with the mouth and lips well shut. It is evident from all that we have just explained that such a voice (in case there exists one) would not be natural but magical, really diabolical'.[21]

Contrary to this, Sir Kenelm Digby in his *Nature of Bodies* (1645) felt that the practice was achieved by sucking the breath inwards. 'In like manner they that are called ventriloqui, do persuade ignorant people that the devil speaketh from within them (deep in their belly). By sucking their breath inwards in a certain manner while they speak whence it followeth that their voice seemeth to come not from them, but from somewhere else hidden within them.'[22]

A Dutch doctor, Conrad Amman, supported this view in his treatises on hearing and speaking, *De Loquela* (1700) stating that ventriloquism was attained by running speech backwards or inhaling rather than exhaling when speaking.[23]

Amman had witnessed the ventriloquism of Babara Jacobi who became somewhat of a celebrity in her home town Haarlem where, in 1645, she astonished observers who crowded into her tiny bedchamber to hear her conversations with her familiar Joachim.[24] Because of her advancing years, Babara Jacobi was confined to her bed where she claimed Joachim also was, and spoke with him on a variety of subjects. Joachim himself was heard to cry, lament, laugh and sometimes sing, to the amazement of all those present. Amman testified that the illusion was so perfect, 'I could have sworn she was talking to her husband two paces at least away. The old woman might easily have passed as a prophetess'.

Barbara Jacobi's seances were considered at the time to be harmless and amusing rather than alarming. However, nearly seventy years later in 1714 on the Island of St. Thomas, a slave was executed for a similar practice. The slave had fashioned a small statue from clay through which he would ventriloquize. His divination was seen by the authorities as diabolical, and he was put to death.[25]

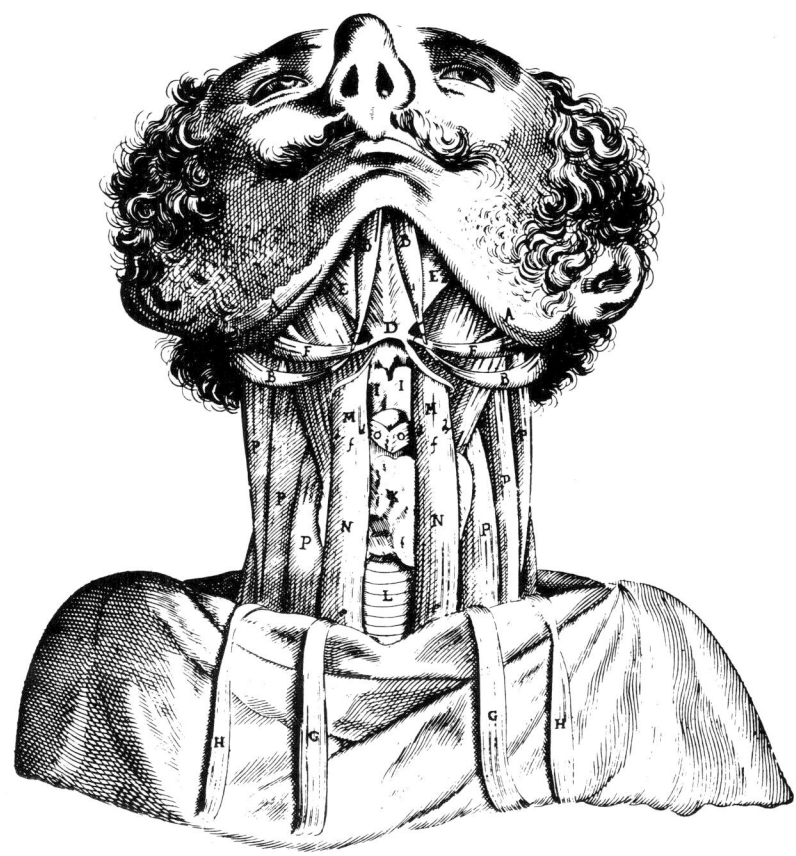

An illustration from Julius Casserius' work on the voice and hearing organs, which became a landmark in anatomical study. Casserius explained ventriloquism as diabolical and magical.

3

COME AND HEAR THE CHANGE OF VOICE

Facing: A full-sized walking figure made by Quisto in 1920. The mouth can be operated either from the shaft beneath the neck or pneumatically from some distance (composite).
Left: A composite figure made by Herbert Brighton in 1940. The mouth and turning head movement are controlled pneumatically.
Right: A sailor-girl figure with mouth movement only, made in 1926 (Papier Mâché). Although the juvenile male figure has dominated the art, in Edwardian times the old lady was a popular character, usually appearing with a male counterpart in a Punch-and-Judy-like situation.

It is evident that few attained and developed the peculiar faculty of ventriloquy. Those who did–while not necessarily employing it for monetary gain or divinatory practice–found it an amusing ability, if only to be used for practical jokes. Such a man was Samuel Honeyman, a blacksmith who lived at Bear Street London, just off Leicester Square, in the early part of the eighteenth century. Honeyman's vocal talent had caused him to be dubbed 'the talking smith', and although in John Byrom's diary[1] he is referred to as 'the famous smith', he is remembered mainly because of his tragic encounter with Thomas Britten.

Thomas Britten was one of the most colorful and fascinating characters of eighteenth-century London.[2] He was a coal merchant by trade, selling small coals from house to house, but it was his love of music that brought him fame. In 1678, above his coal shop in the Clerkenwell district of London, he formed his famous music club, and is credited with being the first person to introduce musical concerts. His house was described by Edward Ward as 'the Athenian tub in Clerkenwell, not much higher than a canary pipe, and the window of his state room not much bigger than the bunghole of a cask'.[3] Yet this humble dwelling did not deter visitors, and his house was frequented by many elite and noted personalities of the day. Among his friends were the

Below: Robert Tattersall with his full-sized figures (1900)

Facing and below: Thomas Britten, 'the small musical coalman' whose death resulted from a ventriloquial hoax.

Duchess of Queensbury, John Hughs the poet, and musicians as famous as Pepusch and the great Mr. Handel, who often played the organ at the club.

Britten's tastes were not confined to music. He was a student of chemistry and an avid collector of old books, his house at the time containing one of the finest collections in England. Towards the end of his life he became very interested in the Rosicrucian philosophy and began to collect a great many books pertaining to the occult.

The circumstances of Britten's death were said to be 'as extraordinary as those of his life'. On a September evening in 1714, his club met for its usual evening of musical delight. To this meeting Mr. Robe, a Middlesex magistrate, brought along Samuel Honeyman, whose presence was unknown to Britten. Like his accomplice, Mr. Robe was a practical joker, but it is doubtful that he or Honeyman could have foreseen the tragic result of their evening's prank. Honeyman began calling Britten in an assumed voice, saying, 'Thomas Britten, prepare to die!'. He went on to say that, unless he repeated the Lord's Prayer three times, he would surely die. Upon hearing this, the terrified coal merchant immediately fell to his knees and did as he was told, but the shock proved too much for him and he was taken to his bed, where he died a few days later. No charge was made against Honeyman for this hoax, probably because of his association with Mr. Robe.

Honeyman performed a similar trick on Dr. Sacherville, a famous political preacher. Although the result was not as tragic as it had been on the previous occasion, it was said to have 'terrified the doctor into near fits'.[4]

While Honeyman preferred to use his talent for practical jokes, many of his contemporaries found they could earn a reasonable living by using their skill for entertainment purposes. A prominent practitioner at the time was Tom King, a 'ventriloquist and lecturer in experimental philosophy', whose performances were attended by most of the fashionable world. During his London exhibitions, a screen was erected between him and the audience. From behind this screen three butchers apparently conversed, a dog barked and knives were sharpened. Finally a calf was heard bleating as it was dragged in, then amidst growling dog and shop talk from the butchers, the audience heard it being slaughtered and hung up. This whole performance was presented to the audience with perfect accuracy, and when the screen was removed, King stood there alone to receive the applause; the butchers, the dog, and the quartered veal had all vanished like a midnight ghost.[5]

Bartholomew Fair: This colorful festivity in eighteenth century London attracted people from all walks of life and brought a diversity of entertainers. Magicians, clowns, puppeteers, jugglers and ventriloquists would perform at the annual event.
The illustration is from a fan leaf based on the painting by Thomas Loggon, the dwarf fan painter (1740).

Below: James Bick, ventriloquist and mimic trumpeteer who performed at the fair during the early part of the eighteenth century.

Below: George Romondo, the ventriloquist and eccentric mimic who was regularly seen at the fair.

A ventriloquist whose stature and appearance caused as much interest as his voice changes was George Romondo. He stood just over three feet tall, wore a large cocked hat, and was known as 'the eccentric mimic'. His acute ear enabled him to imitate instruments, animals and the sawing of wood, often persuading observers that these sounds were proceeding from his pockets or from behind a wall.[9]

Because of his small stature he entered a public house almost unnoticed, then he would suddenly roar like a lion, which usually threw the company into complete alarm. When he had attracted the patrons' attention, he proceeded with his entertainment. He appeared at Bartholomew Fair, as well as in public houses.

In 1750, Mr. Moore advertised himself as 'the wonderful man and child' and 'the curious man in miniature'. His advertisements were sometimes composed in verse:[10]

Hicks Hall in Clerkenwell (1720), which became a popular London coffee house and a frequent haunt for ventriloquial performers.

Facing: A cloth-made talking hand made by Alfred Lemare & Sons in 1895.

> All you that in miracles rejoice,
> Come and hear the change of voice,
> Unto this little fairy haste,
> He never fails to please your taste.

At about the same time as Mr. Moore was displaying his change of voice, Hogarth painted his famous series, 'The Election', in which he showed a small portrait of Sir John Parnell amusing onlookers with his 'talking hand', which has now become a popular feature of ventriloquial entertainment.[11]

In Austria a new dimension was added to the practice of ventriloquism through the talents of the Baron von Mengen. In 1750 he embellished his ventriloquial performances with a small doll figure in which was installed a moving mouth. By moving the mouth and synchronizing these movements with the ventriloquial voice, he gave the effect that the doll itself was talking. The Baron is credited with introducing this marriage between puppetry and ventriloquism which did not become vogue until many years later. At the court in Bayreuth, his amusing and often satirical conversations with his doll were so convincing that an officer who was present during one such performance protested at the inhumane treatment inflicted by the Baron, who finished his entertainment by stuffing the crying doll into his pocket. Being a natural comedian, the Baron seized this opportunity and caused the doll to cry even louder, which brought even stronger protests from the officer. The whole scene evoked howls of laughter from Prince Lichtenstein and other nobles who were present, whereupon the Baron took the doll from his pocket and placed the lifeless figure into the officer's hands. The officer

The frontispiece of the first book on ventriloquism, written by the Abbé de la Chappelle and published in 1772.

examined it, gave it back to the Baron and slid away in embarrassment.

The Baron made no secret of his ventriloquial techniques, and in a letter dated 1770 he explained how he worked. He wrote, 'I press the tongue against the teeth and the left cheek, and the voice seemingly articulated by the doll's mouth really is formed between my mouth, teeth and left cheek. For this purpose, I have to take the precaution of always keeping in reserve a portion of air enough for singing or talking, without the belly or stomach taking part in any manner. This enables me to articulate all the syllables very clearly without any movement of the lips.'[12]

This letter, together with many other items on ventriloquism, was included in *Le Ventriloque ou L'Engastrimythe* by the Abbe de la Chapelle, censor royal at the Lyon and Rouen academies and member of the Royal Society of London. Chapelle's book was the first one on the subject apart from theological works and it dealt not only with the historical background of ventriloquism but also revealed how it was practiced at the time, using the testimony of current exponents. Chapelle's research was aided by Monsieur St. Gille, a grocer from St. Germain-en-Laye, who was reported to be an extraordinary practitioner of *ventriloque*. St. Gille's astonishing talent first engaged the Abbe's interest in the subject, and his book relates many instances of his mentor's clever ventriloquy.

On one occasion, St. Gille was caught in a rainstorm and took shelter in a nearby monastery. Finding the monks at their devotions mourning the loss of a deceased brother, St. Gille began to simulate the distant voice of the departed monk, causing havoc among the clergy. He also used his skill in his shop on certain customers whom he found troublesome.[13]

However, these amusing testimonies were not substantial enough for Chapelle, and he requested the grocer to give him a private demonstration of his craft, to which St. Gille agreed. Both parties sat at a large table, St. Gille at one end and Chapelle at the other. Some time passed before any sound was uttered. Then a voice was heard calling Chapelle by name, which appeared to come from outside. Chapelle then asked the grocer if he were giving a sample of his art, but St. Gille replied only with a smile. Then the voice was heard again, this time apparently coming from beneath the table. As prepared as Chapelle was for this delusion, his senses were completely deceived, and the voices he heard seemed to come from some distance. Chapelle also observed that the ventriloquist remained absolutely mute throughout the whole exercise, with no change in his countenance.[14]

Duly impressed by this display, Chapelle related his testimony to the Royal Academy of Science in Paris, which in consequence requested a further examination, this time to be conducted by commissioners De Fouchi and LeRoi. For this experiment the commissioners, together with the ventriloquist, escorted a certain countess to a spot just outside St. Germain-en-Laye, which had previously been rumored to be haunted. The countess was unaware of the experiment and of St. Gille's ventriloquial skill; consequently, when she heard voices calling her by name, she was convinced that it was an aerial spirit. This experiment also convinced the Royal Academy of Science that the practice of *ventriloque* was able to deceive the human senses.

Chapelle's acute observations revealed for the first time how this feat was achieved. First it was observed that the ventriloquist does not speak from the stomach, as the name implies, but makes the ventriloquial sounds in the same way as sounds are normally produced, except that he diffuses the sound in such a way as to make it appear distant. Further to this, Chapelle noted St. Gille's slow expiration of air, which often caused him to cough after long exertion when the delusion was less perfect. Apart from the change of voice and immobile lips, the author became aware of other factors necessary to produce the ventriloquial illusion. Chapelle noted that the ventriloquist would direct, or rather misdirect, the auditor to the place from which he wished the sound to be heard. This was done very subtly, by a look, a word or a gesture. Chapelle also observed that the experiment carried out upon the countess relied mainly upon the suggestion concerning the aerial spirit. The countess was told that the place to which they were going was haunted. Her acceptance of this was the key to the whole deception.[15]

Le Ventriloque ou L'Engastrimythe, written in Chapelle's native tongue, became the main source of reference to the practice of ventriloquism. It was extraordinary for a book to be written about such an esoteric subject at a time when it had not, as yet, been recognized as an art.

Below: 'The Jugglers' by Jean Louis Hamon. Street entertainers became familiar curiosities in the eighteenth century.

4

FROM THE SAGE TO THE STAGE

Facing: Augustus Peabody (composite) made by Billy Russell in 1940.
Movements: jaw and blinking eyes.

By the late eighteenth century, ventriloquism was becoming established as a recognized entertainment, and many of its exponents often found themselves being patronized by the nobility. Le Sieur Themet was a favorite with the Empress Josephine, advertising himself as an 'imitator and physiomane'. Not only could he change his voice, but also his face, and he had the peculiar ability to laugh on one side of his face and cry on the other. His ventriloquial performance was given in the form of a short sketch in which he was shut up overnight in a mill and imitated the sounds of a hunt outside. The voices of men were heard and the cry of hounds, gradually fading into the distance. This sketch was first presented to an English audience in 1785, when Themet appeared in London.[1]

In the north of England, James Burns, a native of Ireland, was attracting large crowds with his ventriloquial entertainment. Otherwise known as Count O' Burns or Squeaking Tommy, he was frequently seen at the fairs and markets in and around Nottingham, where he exhibited his ventriloquy and imitated various instruments. Burns was a great practical joker, and in 1789, at a market in Nottingham, he began calling a young village girl in the assumed voice of a tiny child who appeared to be in distress. The girl became so distraught at not being able to locate

Below: Female impersonator, Bobby Kimber, with Augustus Peabody. They were chosen for the Royal Command Performance in 1947.

Below: James Burns, the Irish born ventriloquist, who was seen at fairs and races in and around Nottingham in the latter part of the eighteenth century. In his left hand he holds 'Squeaking Tommy,' a small wooden figure through which he would ventriloquize.

the infant that she fainted. At the time the mayor was not amused by this hoax and ordered Burns to spend three days in the local jail.

However this short term did not deter Burns from further employing his skill as a practical joker, as was recorded a few years later at a fish stall in Sheffield. Burns picked up a fish from the stall, shoved his fingers into its gills and asked the stallkeeper if it were fresh.

'I vow to God that it were in the water only yesterday,' was her

reply. The ventriloquist then made a voice appear to come from the fish, at the same time manipulating its mouth, and it said, 'It's a damn lie. I've not seen water for a week.' The woman was so startled that she apparently exercised more care in advertising the freshness of her wares.

In his performances, Burns used a tiny figure that was described as 'an ill-faced doll' which he held wrapped in a linen cloth. From the eighteenth century illustration, it is doubtful whether the figure had any mechanical movement; it appears to be just a crudely carved head on a stick.

Although Burns was known as a 'bird of passage', he made his home in Nottinghamshire. That became his final resting-place when he died on 7 January 1796.[2]

A later print of James Burns published in 1804.

Among the thousands who witnessed Burns' entertainment was Thomas Haskey, a wooden-legged man from neighbouring Staffordshire. Born in Walsall in 1771, Thomas Haskey's first job was as an apprentice to a bridle and bit maker in Bloxwich, but the work proved too mundane for him and he ran away and went into the King's service. While he was in His Majesty's forces, he lost the lower half of his left leg and was subsequently discharged and given a pension. Still in his early twenties, he returned home and for a while took casual employment in Litchfield, where he assisted gardeners by making holes with his wooden leg in which to set potatoes.

During this period, Haskey witnessed the performances of James Burns at the local market-place. It is not known whether Burns and Haskey engaged in any kind of friendship, but the 'Count's' entertainment greatly impressed Haskey, who began imitating him most successfully. His first public display was at a small theatre in Walsall, where, from the gallery, he would 'set the place in an uproar with sham dialogues in two voices'. His reputation grew and he was frequently sent for by Lord Dudley to exhibit his talent for the amusement of His Lordship at Himley.[3]

In spite of Haskey's handicap, he was a smart dresser and his ventriloquial skill was so well developed that he was invited to perform at *Sadler's Wells Theatre* in London. Changing his name from Haskey to Askins, he made his debut on the London stage in the summer of 1796. Although the London audiences were familiar with novel entertainers such as jugglers, magicians, and acrobats, ventriloquism was for many entirely new and still very much a mystery. This must have inspired the management to advertise Askin's entertainment in the following explanatory manner:[4]

Christopher Lee Sugg, 'Professor of Internal Elocution.'
Below: A playbill of Sugg's performance.

These halfpenny tokens were one of the great series issued by tradesmen, politicians, corporations and private individuals to relieve the great deficiency of small change during the latter half of the eighteenth century. There are several varieties of the token, all having the same obverse, but with three different reverses. The first bears an anchor in a circle of leaves, the second a ciphered J.A. within a wreath, and the third the four-line inscription.

Joseph Askins' performances at Sadler's Wells not only established a new entertainment in the theatre, but turned a coffee house and market-day amusement into a respected facet of the performing arts. Due to the growing popularity of the art, many performers began to include it as part of their repertoire, especially those adept in mimicry and impersonation, such as the celebrated actor Charles Mathews in his 'at home' entertainments.

Magicians also began to incorporate this kindred art in their acts, and in 1800 two brothers, Val and Fitz James, presented the best of both. Their program was divided between them, Val providing the magic while Fitz performed the ventriloquism and facial imitations.

Fitz James was a master of the art of ventriloquism. On stage he conversed with a statue that answered him, and also with various invisible people. His most impressive feat was the cry of a watchman gradually approaching. When the cry reached the window James would open it, ask the imaginary watchman the time, receive a reply and close the window. The watchman's cries were heard fading into the distance.[7]

Louis Appollinaire Christien Emmanuel Comte, a native of Geneva, was another magician-ventriloquist. He was once accused of sorcery in his homeland when he caused a voice to ensue from a young pig in the market place. Comte would reenact this incident on stage in a sketch entitled, 'Imitations of Distant Voices'.[8]

In 1810 eccentric performer Christopher Lee Sugg billed himself as 'Professor of Internal Elocution.' Sugg's career spanned between the eighteenth and the nineteenth centuries and he claimed to have taught ventriloquism to the actor Charles Matthews. On the eve of an engagement at Kew, he once found himself faced with a murder charge because of a publicity stunt that he had arranged. Feeling that he needed some sensation to advertise his forthcoming attraction, Sugg had rushed into a baker's shop with a supposedly crying child in his arms; in fact, he had a rag doll wrapped in a blanket. In an apparent rage, Sugg threw the screaming infant into the baker's furnace and ran out of the shop. He was then caught, arrested and taken before the local magistrate, who acquitted him with a small fine and a severe warning.⁹

In America ventriloquism began to enjoy as much popularity as it had in Europe, and the New World gave birth to many fine exponents. One of the first American ventriloquists to gain prominence in his native land was Richard Potter, who was said to be the illegitimate son of Sir Charles Henry Frankland, an English baronet, who was a direct descendant of Oliver Cromwell. His mother, Diana, was a black slave who worked on the Frankland estate. ¹⁰

Potter was born in Boston in 1783 and, despite his illegitimacy, was well provided for by his father, who gave him a good education, eventually sending him to Europe. During this period abroad, he began to learn the ventriloquial art when he became an assistant to John Rannie, a Scottish-born magician. Rannie was particularly proud of his ventriloquial skill and publicly offered 100 guineas to anyone who could equal him.¹¹

Swiss ventriloquist Louis Comte, making a voice come from a pig.

American ventriloquist Jonathan Harrington.

Facing: A playbill of Richard Potter, who became America's first prominent ventriloquial performer.

In 1801, Potter returned to America with Rannie, whom he continued to assist for many years until he eventually embarked upon his own entertainment career and soon established himself as an outstanding performer. His exhibitions were seen by audiences throughout the eastern States for more than twenty years and later inspired the poet John Godfrey Saxe to write, 'I ne'er shall see another show to rank with immortal Potter's.'[12]

Among his various vocal skills was said to be his remarkable imitation of birds. He eventually made his home in Andover where he died on September 20, 1835, at a spot that still bears his

VENTRILOQUISM.

Mr. POTTER,
The VENTRILOQUIST,

Begs leave most respectfully to inform the Ladies and Gentlemen of   that he intends to give an

Evening's Brush to Sweep away
CARE; Or, A Medley to Please,

At Mr.   Ball-Room,
On   Evening,   instant.

In the course of the Evening will be offered upwards of

100
CURIOUS BUT MYSTERIOUS
Experiments,
A SONG,

with Cards, Eggs, Money, &c.

(For Particulars, see small Bills.)

by Mr. POTTER.

PART SECOND.
VENTRILOQUISM.

Mr. P. will display his wonderful but laborious powers of Ventriloquism. He throws his voice into many different parts of the room, and into the gentlemen's hats, trunks, &c. Imitates all kinds of Birds and Beasts, so that few or none will be able to distinguish his imitations from the reality. This part of the performance has never failed of exciting the surprise of the learned and well informed, as the conveyance of sounds is allowed to be one of the greatest curiosities of nature.

PART THIRD.

THE WHOLE TO CONCLUDE WITH A RECITATION AND SONG IN CHARACTER OF TIMOTHY NORPOST.

Alexandre Vattermare, the French ventriloquist.

Facing: A playbill of Vattermare's entertainment in which he portrayed all thirteen characters.

name–Potters Place, New Hampshire.

Potter was succeeded by a native of Boston, Jonathan Harrington, who gained prominence during the years preceding the Civil War and was quoted by the press as 'the greatest ventriloquist in America'.[13]

In 1820, through the talent of a young Frenchman, the art was elevated to a new plane. Nicholas Marie Alexandre Vattermare was undoubtedly the most celebrated ventriloquists of the period. Born in Paris at the turn of the century, his ventriloquial ability was developed at an early age and at eleven he entertained Napoleon Bonaparte. After schooling, his parents persuaded him to take up a medical career and he became a surgeon at the St. Louis hospital in Paris. It was there that his extraordinary ventriloquial ability began to unnerve his fellow colleagues, when many of the corpses were heard to speak. Soon this aptitude outweighed his skill as a surgeon and he turned to a theatrical career, entertaining throughout Europe.

In 1820 Vattermare brought his entertainment to Britain where he billed himself as Monsieur Alexandre, performing in every major city and town throughout the UK and eventually being summoned to appear before the Royal family.

His talent seemed to exceed those of his predecessors. He could

ADELPHI THEATRE, STRAND.

OPEN MONDAY, TUESDAY, THURSDAY, and SATURDAY.

Monsieur ALEXANDRE,
The celebrated Dramatic Ventriloquist,

Will deliver, an entirely New Comic, Characteristic, Vocalic, Mimetic, Multiformical, Maniloquous, Ubiquitarical ENTERTAINMENT, in Three Parts, (in ENGLISH) constructed expressly for this Occasion, and entitled THE

Adventures of a Ventriloquist,
OR, THE ROGUERIES OF NICHOLAS.

In which he will display the various astonishing Vocal Illusions, for which he has been so justly celebrated and distinguished on the Continent, and which have been represented with such signal Approbation, before most of the Crowned Heads and Princes of Europe.

Mons. A. being a Native of Paris, it is hoped *French Leave* will be granted to any Peculiarities of Pronunciation in the English Language, that may be *found absent*.

PERSONÆ OF THE ENTERTAINMENT.
VISIBLE PERSONS.

ALDERMAN PILLBURY, an Invalid of his own making, dieting on the Pharmacopœia, and suffering under a complication of Patent Medicines, two Doctors, an Apothecary, and his Wife!

CAPTAIN FURLOUGH, a young Officer of Infantry, on the Home Service, shewing the height to which a Lover's Flame may carry him, by ascending his Mistress's Chimney.

NICHOLAS, Servant to the Alderman, with an appetency to Accident, in breaking every thing he lays his hand on, but invariably mending matters through an Ingenuity sharpened with Hunger, and assisted by Opportunity.

Mrs. PILLBURY, Wife of the Alderman, a Lady strongly impressed with an Idea that Prevention is better than Cure, and with a real annoying fondness for her Spouse, admirably illustrating the secret of killing with kindness.

Miss FLIRTILLA PILLBURY, Daughter of the Alderman, beloved by the Captain. As this young Lady is under Seventeen, her Character, it may be expected, is not yet settled; her Ideas, however, are strongly fixed on having a young Officer of Infantry for her Husband, and living in a Cottage near some *Nursery* Grounds---with a Nunnery and the Serpentine in perspective, in the event of disappointment.

INVISIBLE PERSONS.

ANDREW STUMP, Surgeon Dentist and Trepanner, getting his Bread by other People's Teeth, and holding tight what he does get; his Generosity being confined to giving---Advice. NOT TO BE SEEN on account of a violent Pain in his Jaws, which defies his own Specific, and confines him to his Room.

JACOB, his Man, with a very broad back, as amiable as his Master, and hoping to be a great Drawer in time, practising meanwhile on the Corks, kept in the dark by Nicholas, but still getting something for his pains. NOT TO BE SEEN on account of being in the Cellar all the time.

PILLBURY MINIMUS, an Infant in Arms, with a fine Voice for Tragedy. NOT TO BE SEEN from the intervention of a Cradle, and breaking through the desirable consummation of Children being seen and not heard.

ASSUMED PERSONS.

SQUIRE TIVY, possessing all the good Qualities of a Country Fox-hunter, viz. a Love of Sport and good Lungs.

NICK TONGS, a young Beginner, taking the place of his Master to try his hand at a pull.---Drawing all but the right, and only charging for one.

IMITATED HALF-LENGTH PERSONS.

CELESTINE, a young Novice, learning to sing, but wanting an Ear and a Voice.

SISTERS MUMBLE, DOLEFUL, JOLIE, SNUFFLE, LAMBERTE, and **SURLY**, characteristically Toothless, Melancholy, Giddy, Snuffy, Fat, and Disfigured.

QUADRUPEDS, &c.

Growler, the Alderman's Dog---Givetongue, another Dog, a Friend of his---Felina, Mrs. Pillbury's Cat---Gobble, a Turkey Cock---a Pig and Sow with their Family---a Cock and three Hens, Ducks, Drakes, &c

INANIMATE OBJECTS, &c.

An Omelet frying---a Flint and Steel---a Plane---a Saw---a Corkscrew---a Stick---and a Guitar.

SYNOPSIS OF THE ENTERTAINMENT.
PART I.
FOOD AND PHYSIC.
CUPID TURNED CHIMNEY SWEEP.

Necessity shewn to be the Mother of Invention, and Mrs. Glasse (without any reflections) outdone by a visible Recipe for preparing a Dish, that in point of cheapness and facility, is superior to any thing in the "whole Art of Cookery".

In this Part, for the Amusement of the Curious, the following *PARADOXES*, are satisfactorily proved, viz.

That Board Wages are a bare Cupboard	That Omelets may be made without Eggs, and fried without Fire
That Beet Root is a better specific for a sudden Hoarseness than candied Horehound	That Debts may be paid without Disbursement, and
That a Workman may be something without his Tools	That a Man may give another verbal leave of Absence, without knowing it

PART II.
WINE AND THE TOOTH ACHE,
OR, THE BITER BIT.

In which Monsr. A. will perform one of the Acts of the Bottle Conjuror, by Drinking and Singing at the same time. He will also hold a Conversation in a Cellar, and yet not be---low.

In this Part the following further *PARODOXES* for the continued Amusement of the Curious, are proved, viz.

That a Man may be a Dentist, and no Tooth Drawer	That what is good for the Goose is not always good for the Gander
That there is Virtue in having a Cold	That self-taught Artists are not always the best---and
That a Trap Door may be made an Interpreter, and convey one word for another	That it is not always advantageous to be only charged one sixth of the price of a thing.

PART III.
CURTAIN LECTURES.
JACK IN THE BOX.

Containing a Keyhole Illustration of Domestic Felicity, and a small Peep behind the Grate, or the Sisterhood *unveiled*, together with a new method of playing at Bumble Puppy.

The *PARADOXES* proved in this Part, are chiefly these, that

There may be Sporting without Hunting,	That five Persons may be here, there, everywhere, and no where, at the same Time.
That we may get the Horns without catching the Stag,	
That a Man may signify his Will against his Will, and	

The Whole Embodied, Illustrated, and Delivered by MONSIEUR ALEXANDRE.

⁂ Between each Part, a SELECT BAND, led by Mr. PARNELL, will perform the most celebrated Symphonies of Mozart, Haydn, Beethoven, &c. arranged as Quintetts expressly for this Occasion.

The LOCALE of the Entertainment painted by Messrs. FRANKLIN and CARROLL.---The DRESSES by Mr. and Miss GODBEE.

In consequence of the numerous Enquiries continually making for the next Representation of the ORIGINAL Piece of TOM and JERRY produced at this Theatre, the Public are respectfully informed, that it cannot be played again till October next.

BOX, 4s. PIT, 2s. GALLERY, 1s. Doors open at 7, and commence at 8. No Money returned. [W. GLINDON, Printer, Rupert Street.

not only imitate every audible animate sound but also inanimate ones, such as the sawing of wood or the frying of an omelette. He was also adept as a quick-change artist and in 1822, at London's *Adelphi Theatre*, he presented 'The Adventures of a Ventriloquist', subtitled 'The Rogueries of Nicholas'[14] in which he portrayed all thirteen characters, rapidly changing his face and costume for each. Vattermare achieved this feat by assuming the voices of various characters who appeared to be conversing with him from off-stage. When he made an exit as one character, he would rapidly change his costume, conversing in several voices at the same time and giving the impression that there was another room from which the characters were making their exits and entrances. He produced the effect of persons speaking from behind a door, inside a trunk, from the chimney and the cellar with precision and accuracy.

The anecdotes related about him were numerous. At one time in the Strand, he caused a traffic jam by making a distressed voice call from a passing hay cart. Pedestrians would not let the driver proceed until they had unloaded all the hay, only to find that their efforts were in vain.

Vattermare not only gained the respect and admiration of the thousands who flocked to see him, but also of various eminent people of the day. When he entertained Sir Walter Scott at Abbotsford, the poet and novelist was so impressed that he wrote a short verse for him, in which he called him the 'arch deceiver':[15]

Facing: Alexandre Vattermare's production 'Devil on Two Sticks', illustrating many of the characters he portrayed through his rapid voice and costume changes.

Of yore in old England, it was not thought good
To carry two visages under one hood:
What should folks say to you, who have faces such plenty,
That from under one hood, you last night showed us twenty?
Stand forth, arch deceiver! and tell the truth,
Are you handsome or ugly? In age or youth?
Man, woman, or child? Or a dog or a mouse?
Or are you, at once, each live thing in a house?
Each live thing, did I ask? each dead implement too!
A workshop in your person, saw, chisel, and screw,
Above all, are you one individual? I know
You must be at least, Alexandre & Co.
But I think you're a troop–an assembly–a mob,
And that I, as the Sheriff, must take up the job,
And instead of rehearsing your wonders in verse
Must read you the Riot-Act, and bid you disperse.

Having received world acclaim as a ventriloquial entertainer, Vattermare turned his energies towards more academic

PORTRAITS OF MONS^R. ALEXANDRE,
IN HIS VARIOUS CHARACTERS OF THE
ROGUERIES OF NICHOLAS.

endeavours. He devoted himself to a mission to promote and establish free libraries around the world through a system of international exchanges. This scheme, known as Vattermare's System of International Exchanges, was designed to give the intellectual treasures of the art world the same circulation as commerce had already given its material ones. His idea was cultivated during his travels as an entertainer when he would frequent libraries and museums, often finding duplicates of books 'looked upon as mere rubbish in one city while regarded as indispensable in another'. His plan was to exchange this surplus of cultural wealth between countries.

However, his idealistic scheme met with staunch opposition. One critic wrote, 'His system of international exchanges is

Above: The Boston Public Library, the establishment of which was largely due to the efforts of Alexandre Vattermare and his relentless campaign to form a free public library in Boston. His gift of fifty books from Paris to the City of Boston formed the basis of the present library.

Right: A vignette taken of Vattermare when he was 60.

Facing: The characters performed by Vattermare on the London stage in 1820.

A playbill of Mr. Jacobs' 'The Royal Ventriloquist.'

thought to be a substitute for his worn-out voice of ventriloquism'. In spite of such harsh criticism, Vattermare continued his campaigning and shortly after he arrived in America he presented his scheme to the government. President Van Buren was delighted with his plan and so were the most prominent political leaders. Consequently, in February 1840, Congress passed a resolution giving authority to the librarian to exchange such duplicates as might be in the Library of Congress. It was also decided that fifty additional copies of each volume of documents should be printed for exchange in foreign countries.

When he arrived in Boston in 1841, Vattermare found, as he had elsewhere, that there was no public institution to advocate his scheme. He began campaigning to establish a free public library which not only attracted the attention of the people of Boston but gained the support of the mayor, Josiah Quincey, whom Vattermare persuaded with visits and letters. Vattermare presented a small gift of fifty books from the city of Paris to the city of Boston, which formed the basis of the Public Library of Boston.[16]

His efforts were summed up by Justin Windsor's *History of Boston* when he wrote, 'Whatever we think of Vattermare, whether we call him an enthusiast or something worse or better, we must recognize his contagious energy which induced state after state to succumb to his representations so that by 1853, he had brought one hundred and thirty libraries within his operations, and between 1847 and 1851 he had brought from France for American libraries 30,655 volumes, besides maps, engravings, etc.' Although Vattermare's exchange system gradually lost favor, he continued his campaigning until shortly before his death in France in 1864.[17]

Vattermare's success prompted a new interest in his art, and many performers began staging one-man shows. Mr. Jacobs, a magician, billed himself as 'the royal ventriloquist', and presented a short play called 'Alderman Gobble and his Curious Family'. Although this was a facsimile of Vattermare's 'Rogueries of Nicholas', Jacobs was accomplished in the art and his ventriloquy was said to have exceeded his conjuring talents.[18]

Another magician-ventriloquist was George Sutton who, like many of his contemporaries, had more than one string to his bow. In the course of his evening's entertainment he would 'display an experiment in Egyptian sorcery, play several airs on two jews' harps, make a lady disappear from the audience, and introduce a speaking automaton.' The automaton was a small figure that moved its lips by the operation of a spring mechanism.

George Sutton, who employed a speaking automaton through which he would ventriloquize. During his performance his vocal organs were so well controlled that he would hold a candle to his lips without disturbing the flame with his breath.

Sutton used this to illustrate the oracles of antiquity and the responses from the figure were delivered by him ventriloquially.

During a trip to America, Sutton wrote a small book entitled 'A *Treatise on Ventriloquism*'. This book, published in 1833, is one of the earliest works written by a ventriloquist about his art and is probably one of the rarest on the subject. Sutton was a success on both sides of the Atlantic, making a tour of the principal cities of the USA.[19]

5

VOCAL GYRATIONS

Facing: During the early variety era, black figures were extensively employed by ventriloquial artists. The characters they embodied were derived from the popular minstrel shows. These two wooden knee figures were made in the nineteen twenties. The figure on the left, made by W. Shaw, has a mouth movement only. The other figures with eyes and drop jaw movement; was made by Revello Pettee.

Ventriloquism had become a familiar amusement by the middle of the nineteenth century, although its practice was still misunderstood. Many believed that the ventriloquist was endowed with a supernatural gift that enabled him to 'throw his voice'. This expression, which had become a catch-phrase associated with the art, was largely propagated by Henry Cockton's novel *The Life and Adventures of Valentine Vox the Ventriloquist.*[1] Unlike his many real-life contemporaries, Valentine Vox did not indulge his talent for stage presentation, but instead constantly performed superhuman ventriloquial feats that either confused the populace or managed to save the day. First published in 1840, the book became extremely popular. The *London Times* said; 'It would keep the most melancholy reader in side-shaking fits of laughter'. It was delightfully illustrated with sixty pictures by Thomas Onwyn.[2]

Although Henry Cockton wrote very little about the art or about ventriloquists themselves, it is evident that he drew much of his inspiration from the numerous anecdotes related about them, in particular those concerning Alexandre Vattermare.

The most prominent exponent of ventriloquism to appear during this period was William Edward Love,[3] who preferred to call himself a 'polyphonist'. His powers of mimicry were said to

Below: Alex Davies with his black figures in 1890.

Valentine Vox as he appeared in the original novel by Henry Cockton in 1840. Valentine (third from right) mischievously throws his voice up the chimney.

Below: A later version of Cockton's character illustrated in the reprint of his book in 1881.

be on a par with those of Vattermare, who had set a precedent in the art. Love was born in England in 1806, and began to experiment with ventriloquism at the age of ten during his schooling at Nelson House, Wimbledon. He first employed his talent to deceive his fellow-pupils during an escapade in the headmaster's orchard. Love had been given the duty of lookout in case the gardener should return unexpectedly, and he began to mimic the angry shout of the gardener completely deceiving his fellow students who dropped the apples and fled. This incident prompted Love to experiment further with his vocal organs and, by the time he was twelve, he had become quite proficient at imitating the various sounds of machinery and inanimate objects. In fact, he would attempt to mimic any sound that struck his ear.

Love became a professional performer in 1826 and began touring the principal towns in the UK. He made his first London appearance at the *Assembly Rooms* in 1834, eventually touring Europe and later America. He was at the zenith of his fame in the 1850s, during which time he presented his novel entertainment under such titles as 'Love's Labor's Lost', 'Love in All Shapes',

William Edward Love, polyphonist and ventriloquist.

Frederic Maccabe, musician, composer and ventriloquist.

and 'Love's Lubrication'.[4]

Love's performances were more than mere demonstrations of his ventriloquial ability. The *New York Star* said, 'We cannot, without injustice, class him with the mere ordinary mimic and ventriloquist, whose performances too frequently consist of a monotonous mass of pointless dialogue. His entertainments are embellished by taste, humor, wit, and sentiment.'

Like Vattermare, Love could change his face as well as his voice, and his impersonations of various characters were one of the highlights of his entertainment. His ability was summed up by one newspaper which said, 'His ventriloquism is as perfect as any recorded in the annals of the art.'[5]

In 1858, tragedy struck this brilliant artist when he suddenly contracted paralysis. His illness, unfortunately, never allowed him to perform again and nine years later, on March 16, 1867, he died at his home in the Strand.

Prominent successors of Love were W. S. Woodin and Frederic Maccabe. Woodin was the founder of the *Polygraphic Hall* that eventually became the *Charing Cross Theatre*, where he gave ventriloquial and character impressions in the form of short sketches.

G. W. Jester who challenged Maccabe to a ventriloquial duel.

Another platform for this type of entertainment was 'The Home of Mystery', *Egyptian Hall*, Piccadilly. This was the mecca for the pseudo-occult performing arts, presenting ventriloquists, jugglers, illusionists and magicians from around the world. It was there that Frederick Maccabe first gained public favor in a show presented by Professor Anderson as 'the wizard of the north.' Maccabe, a small genial man, was a multi-talented performer, possessing all the necessary requisites for successful entertainment. He was a fine composer and musician and could manage his flexible voice with equal skill as a singer, mimic and ventriloquist. He used his various talents in a one-man show entitled 'Begone Dull Care'.[6]

In 1869 during a week's engagement at *St James Hall*, Maccabe was informed that another ventriloquist had arrived to 'accept his challenge'. The other ventriloquist was G. W. Jester, 'the man with the talking hand'.[7] Jester, an Anglo-Frenchman, was a prominent performer at the time. The challenge he accepted was an advertisement in the *Era* which stated, 'Maccabe challenges the world as a ventriloquist.'

Taking this publicity literally, Jester proposed a ventriloquial contest between himself and Maccabe, to be judged by an independent panel. Maccabe, however, declined to accept the proposal, claiming that to win would be a barren victory, adding

WYMAN,
THE CELEBRATED
American Ventriloquist
AND
WIZARD,
Is now making a Tour of the United States.

In the various departments of his line of business, he is unrivalled. As a
MAGICIAN,
He is not surpassed, if equalled, by any talent in the country, foreign or otherwise, while as a
VENTRILOQUIST,..
He is admitted to be the best now before the public. His life-moving and speaking
AUTOMATONS,
Also afford the utmost delight and amusement to all Altogether, WYMAN'S ENTERTAINMENT is of the most wonderful and at the same time, laughter-provoking character.
☞ See WYMAN by all means, when the opportunity offers.

WYMAN'S HAND-BOOK OF MAGIC,
Explaining all the tricks performed by Anderson, Blitz, Adrian, McAllister, Alexander, Heller and others, can be had of Mr. Wyman, or of
T. W. STRONG, 98 Nassau-st., N. Y..
Either at wholesale or retail. 578,000 copies of this popular work has been sold within the last three years.

A playbill of John Wyman, who proudly billed himself as 'The American Ventriloquist'.

nothing to his pocket or reputation. He further stated that a skilful ventriloquist creates his illusion with the least possible movement of his mouth and that, if he were to engage in such a contest, he would have to insist that Mr. Jester shave off his large imperial moustache!

Love, Maccabe, and Vattermare were all masters of the ventriloquial art during the nineteenth century. They could conjure up sounds that gave to the audience imaginary pictures of where they were coming from, or from whom. The cries of animals were heard, the drone of insects and the movements of inanimate objects. They could make voices come from without and within, above and below. These artists required no props or special settings, but through their ventriloquial ability alone the stage would become full of objects, animals and people.

This distant voice ventriloquism is the most skilful facet of the art. It is therefore understandable that many performers who had mastered the art to such a degree frowned upon the use of automatons, feeling that they reduced ventriloquism to a sideshow amusement. William Love felt that ventriloquial figures gave a 'primitive illusionary effect'[8] and had no place in the polished entertainment that he and his contemporaries presented.

Nevertheless, automatons were becoming increasingly popular and many artists began incorporating them in their performances. In America both Signor Blizt and John Wyman employed them in their entertainment. Signor Blizt also imitated various distant voices, the buzz of an invisible bee and the convincing crying of a baby. The automaton he used was named Bobby.[9]

At about the same time John Wyman, a native of America, proudly billed himself as 'the American ventriloquist', becoming a foremost entertainer of his day. On five separate occasions he was summoned to perform at the White House for Presidents Fillmore and Lincoln.[10]

The one-man shows which were being presented during the middle of the nineteenth century gradually gave way to the new institution of family variety entertainment. Music hall or vaudeville became the new challenge to the entertainer. It was competitive, and the limited time allowed to each performer whittled down extraneous dialogue and labored material until what was left was the essence of a performer's worth.

The marriage of puppetry and ventriloquism proved attractive in this type of entertainment, in spite of the fact that many figures were crudely made and very often grotesque. The mouth-moving

E. D. Davies, who pioneered ventriloquy in the halls, with his two speaking dolls Tommy and Joey.

automatons gradually became synonymous with the art and the ventriloquist and his 'speaking dolls', as they were called, were soon a fixture of variety entertainment.

The pioneer of ventriloquy in the music halls was E. D. Davies, born in Ireland in 1836. At fifteen he made his stage debut at the *Queens Theatre*, Dublin, appearing as a comedian-ventriloquist and billed as 'the Dublin boy'. A few years later he introduced a new entertainment entitled, 'The Anecdotes and Adventures of the Funniest of Funny Folks', in which he used two fully-dressed knee figures, Tommy and Joey. Davies would sit these mouth-moving dolls on his knees and not only cause them to speak but also sing 'in a manner rivalling the celebrated songsters of the day'. His entertainment was further embellished by jigs, songs and distant voice technique as he spoke to imaginary persons behind the curtain, upstairs and inside a box.[11]

The addition of the ventriloquial figure increased the popularity of the art and, during the latter half of the nineteenth century, numerous ventriloquists began to appear on the scene. Many of these artists accompanied themselves with a family of figures which became commonly known as 'the row', and the performer would move from one to the next, delivering a certain amount of dialogue through each.

The most successful ventriloquist to appear during the music hall era was Lieutenant Walter Cole, who topped the variety bills for more than thirty years (1870-1900), playing to audiences around the world. Like many exponents of the art, Cole began practicing ventriloquism at school and claimed that much of his ability was inherited from his mother, an amateur ventriloquist. At his school in the Old Kent Road, he would often imitate the distant horn of the approaching stagecoach, which never failed to make the teacher check his watch.

Cole earned his title of Lieutenant, serving in the Royal Navy for more than eight years, where he continued to exercise his ventriloquial talent by entertaining the ship's officers and crew. When he returned to civilian life he became a professional entertainer, first appearing under the name of DeLacey, but later reverting to his own name and using his naval title.[12]

In his presentation 'Merry Folks,' Cole credited himself with being the first to introduce life-sized figures that walked as well as talked. His family or 'row' of figures was a colorful group of characters, each one bearing its own stamp of individuality. There was his old man and woman, Tommy Treddlehoyle and Maggie MacDougall, who argued continuously amid Cole's interjections, and the sombre Quaker Zachariah, evoking laugh-

A programme of Lieutenant Walter Cole, the most prominent exponent of the art during the latter part of the nineteenth century.

Facing: A poster of Coles entertainment 'Merry Folks'

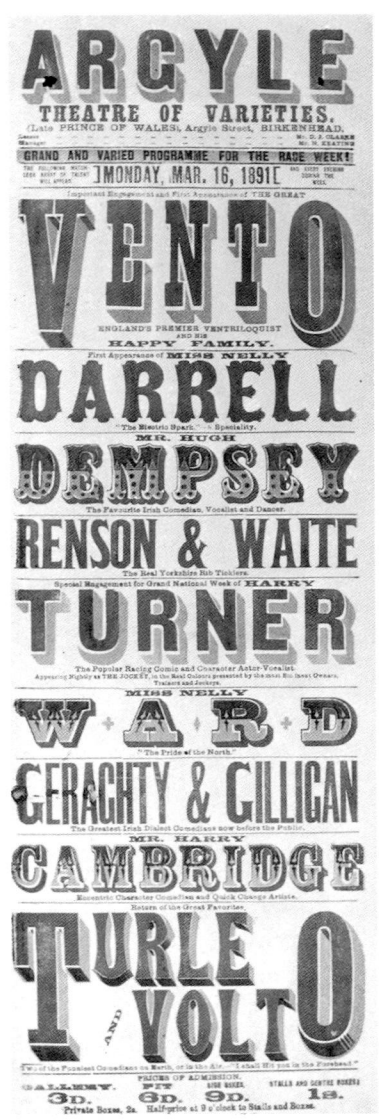

Facing: Harry Vento, whose varied entertainment involved many novel items, included a talking clock in his 'Squire of Haslemere' production.

ter with his drawn-out speeches. Another figure was the boozy and irrepressible Ally Sloper, who proved to be one of Cole's most popular characters. The papers said, 'Nothing we have seen in the ventriloquial art can excel or even approach this latest novelty, wonderfully lifelike in appearance and speech.' However, Cole's favorite character with his audiences was his little girl, Julia Sweet, who would appear wearing a dainty dress and would sing, 'Lay me down in my little cot.' On stage Julia would fidget, claiming that she was sitting on a pin, which Cole would deny as nonsense. Her reply became a favorite catchphrase with the audience, 'If you were sitting where I am sitting, you'd soon know, Mr. Cole!'[13]

Cole was also proficient in distant voice technique and would converse with the invisible character James Anderson on the roof. He also imitated the cries of animals. His polished entertainment was well received both in America and in Europe, where he would often perform in the language of the country in which he appeared.

Cole's most prominent rival was Frank Travis, 'the society ventriloquist', who gained fame in 1879 after a successful tour of the Continent. Travis, a Yorkshireman, appeared on stage in a military uniform and assumed the title of Lieutenant. He employed seven ventriloquial figures which he would seat around a table, singing and conversing through each in turn. These were supplemented by a walking figure of a Crimean veteran who would sing, with Travis's assistance, 'The Boys of the Old Brigade'. While ventriloquizing, it was said that 'Travis maintained immobile lips throughout' and further enhanced his performances by smoking and drinking from a glass of beer.[14]

Although lip control remained the impressive feat of the ventriloquist, its importance appeared to be overshadowed by the 'speaking dolls' which were not only becoming lifelike but lifesized, with many possessing a variety of complicated movements.

Ventriloquists jealously guarded the secrets of their figures and would often patent their designs. They also attempted to protect their presentations. In 1883, a personal battle ensued between Frank Millis and Frank Travis. Millis, an Australian, had gained himself a prominent place in British music hall and his act featured a number of novel figures, his principal being Terence O'Reilly, a red-headed Irish doll.[15] In an advertisement which he placed in a leading theatrical paper, Millis accused Travis of stealing his crying baby idea (a feature, incidentally, that Vattermare had included in his entertainment some sixty years

Frank Travis with a small hand figure.

Facing: Ventriloquiste is the noun given to female practitioners of the art. Madeline Rosa, an Englishwoman, made her début at the Folies Bergère in 1881. Her husband, Frank Travis, known as 'the society ventriloquist,' taught her the fundamentals of the art.

Ed Reynard, the American Vaudeville ventriloquist.

earlier). Millis also challenged Travis to a wager of £10 if he could find anything in his act that was not completely original. Continuously conscious of this 'brain picking', Millis often underlined his advertisements with the phrase 'more ideas for imitators shortly'.

In spite of the jealousies and occasional mud-slinging, the search for novelty continued, resulting in numerous unique presentations. Harry Vento in his 'Squire of Haslemere' production introduced life-sized figures of famous music hall artists such as George Chirwin, Charles Coburn, Lottie Collins and Dan Leno. Vento was the proprietor of *Vento Varieties* in Portsmouth, which eventually became the *People's Palace Theatre*.[16]

Another novel production was Fred Neiman's Ventriloquial Minstrels. Eight figures filled the stage, dressed in the traditional minstrels' attire and through the voice of them all gave a complete minstrel show, the movements of the figures operated by a complicated system of bulbs, wires and tubes. Neiman, who made his debut in 1876, also produced a 'Ventriloquial Parliament', which included figures of Gladstone, Beaconsfield and Lord Randolph Churchill.[17]

One of the most outstanding novelties was presented by Carl

Below: Fred Nieman with his ventriloquial minstrels.

Nobel of Copenhagen. It was a clever visual as well as vocal illusion, giving the appearance of three people balancing on top of each other. The ventriloquist was in the middle carrying on his shoulders the figure of a Frenchman, while below an old woman hobbled along, appearing to carry the load.[18]

In 1881 the art was given a feminine touch when a pretty English woman, Madeline Rosa, made her stage debut at the *Folies Bergere* in Paris, billing herself as the 'world's first lady ventriloquist'. In her act she skilfully manipulated six figures, and her attractive appearance, coupled with such novel entertainment, soon saw her the toast of Paris. Miss Rosa, who had learned her craft from her husband Frank Travis, went on to perform in Europe's principal cities and eventually appeared in London and America.[19]

In the USA Harry Kennedy, Ed Reynard and A. O. Duncan were among the most celebrated vaudeville ventriloquists of the late 19th century. English-born Harry Kennedy's presentation, 'The Ventriloquist's Dream', was well-received on both sides of the Atlantic, although he became more famous as a composer of songs, the most noted being 'Say Au Revoir'.[20] At the time, Ed Reynard was quoted by the press as 'America's greatest ventrilquist'. His production 'Morning in Hicksville' was an elaborate act, sumptuously staged, showing a cottage exterior, and his many figures which seemed to move by themselves appeared from various parts of the stage.[21]

A. O. Duncan also used a group of figures, often incorporating them in political sketches. Duncan preferred to call the art of ventriloquism 'vocal gyrations'.[22]

Carl Nobel featuring his clever visual act, which seemed to be three people balancing on one another.

6

PINOCCHIO BECOMES A BOY

Facing: Although Arthur Prince's Jim and Fred Russell's Joe were original character creations, the heads of the figures were taken from the same mould as this one made by Alfred Lemare in 1895. (composite).

Although variations were often introduced, the use of a group or row of figures was the accepted format for the ventriloquial act. However, in 1896, this familiar pattern was changed when a young man named Fred Russell walked on to the stage of London's *Palace Theatre*, carrying a single figure which he sat on his knee. The dummy, an impudent coster-monger named Joe, immediately captured the audience with his brazen Cockney humor. This form of presentation, using a single knee figure, changed the ventriloquial style of entertainment, and Fred Russell became known as the 'father of modern ventriloquism.'[1]

His enormous success was due not only to his pioneering the use of a single figure; more important was his format, a pattern that most ventriloquists have followed ever since. Dispensing with the row and displays of technique, Fred Russell presented a fast-moving double act with himself playing the straight man, or feed, to Coster Joe, elevating his sidekick to a place of prominence, a place that ventriloquial figures have held over their human partners ever since. From this point on the personality of the figures overshadowed that of the ventriloquists whose vocal skills became subordinate to their animated partners. Like the story of Pinnochio in which the character eventually stopped telling lies and became a real boy, ventriloquial figures began to

A.C. Astor with his boy figure made by Alfred LeMare.

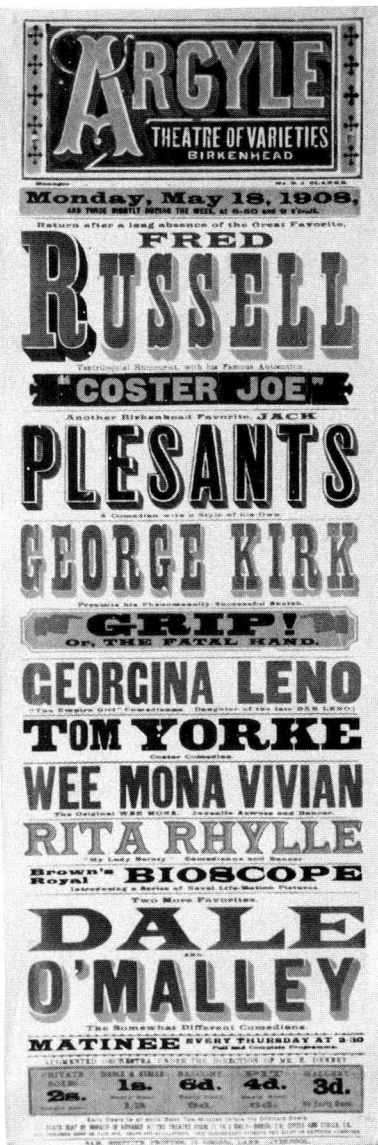

emerge as real personalities. Fred Russell went on to become one of the most celebrated individuals in the world of variety entertainment.

He was born Thomas Frederic Parnell on September 2, 1862. During his schooldays, he was inspired by the book *Valentine Vox* and began entertaining as an amateur. When he left school he secured a job in the newspaper business and in 1894, after several years' apprenticeship, became the editor of the *Kingsland and Hackney Gazette*. However, he was still an enthusiastic ventriloquist and during the evenings would earn extra guineas by entertaining at private functions. He occasionally appeared at the *Crystal Palace*, using an orthodox 'row' of figures.

Smoking-room concerts were fashionable at the time and, in order to accommodate to the needs of a smaller area, he began using a single figure, Coster Joe, named after a song by vaudevillian The Great Vance. In 1896 he was one of the entertainers at a large dinner attended by Charles Morton, who had come out of retirement to run the *Palace Theatre*. Impressed by the young ventriloquist, Morton offered him a trial engagement at £10 a week. Parnell accepted and, changing his name to Russell after his local MP Sir Charles Russell, he made his debut at the *Palace Theatre* on March 6, 1896. Over the next two years, Fred Russell with his homunculus Coster Joe appeared at the theatre almost continuously, causing the ventriloquist to abandon his newspaper career altogether. His specialty was making up impromptu rhymes suggested by the audience and, although he did not use the traditional 'row', he occasionally staged productions engaging as many as eighteen figures. The most popular of these scenas was 'Breach of Promise' with himself playing the counsel for the defense.

Fred Russell not only gained a world-wide reputation as an outstanding performer, but was highly respected within the profession, where he continuously endeavored to improve the interests and working conditions of his fellow artists. In 1906 he was a key figure in establishing the Variety Artist Federation and in the same year founded its official organ, *The Performer*, continuing as its managing director for thirty years.

It was largely due to his efforts to improve conditions in the profession that established a satisfactory charter which still governs variety contracts today. He took part in the 1932 Royal Variety Performance and, although he intended to retire at seventy, he continued to make appearances and in the early 1950s was seen several times on television.

Further acknowledged as 'the father of variety', Fred Russell

Fred Russell, who was dubbed 'the father of modern ventriloquism', with his knee figure, Coster Joe.

On the sands, the Punch and Judy man adds a new feature to his traditional entertainment.

was given every honor that his colleagues could bestow and in 1954, in recognition of his long years in the profession, he was awarded the OBE.

Until his death in 1957[2] at the age of ninety-five, he not only possessed all his faculties but maintained the impressive dignity and quick wit that had originally brought him to fame. At a birthday celebration shortly before his death, he recalled the early advice of his father to 'keep his mouth shut'. 'So,' he added, 'I became a ventriloquist'.[3]

By the 1900s the single figure method seemed to increase the number of ventriloquial performers and soon the ventriloquist and his 'familiar' were not only seen on almost every variety bill, but hundreds began appearing at fairs and coastal resorts that had so far been dominated by the Punch and Judy men. These beach entertainers would hire a small pitch for a few shillings and perform daily, in the hope that the weather would be fine and the sun worshippers generous enough to deposit a few coppers into a hat. For many this was casual summer labor–for others it marked the beginning of a professional career.

A figurine of a pierrot ventriloquist (1910).

In keeping with the growing popularity of the art, this song 'Bread and Butter' was published in 1927.

Besides the buskers who strolled the sands at the British coastal resorts, the colorful pierrot troupes often featured a ventriloquial artiste in their repertory. Below: The Catlin Royal Pierrots who appeared at Yarmouth in 1913.

On the sands at Morecambe, a young Yorkshire lad, Tommy Whitaker, entertained holidaymakers with a small knee figure given to him by his uncle. These crude performances were the beginning of a career that eventually saw him entertaining at the top of variety programs throughout the world under the pseudonym Coram. After touring the music halls for many years in the north of England, Coram eventually made his London debut in 1905 with his doll Jerry Fisher in a sketch entitled 'The Joys of a Motorist'. As the curtain rose, Jerry was seen sitting by himself on a stile, then Coram drove on to the stage in an automobile. During the dialogue that followed, Coram sat in the car the whole time, operating the figure's movements by a compressed air mechanism. After a lively exchange of patter, Coram eventually drove off-stage, leaving Jerry to receive the applause.[4]

This spectacle made an immediate impact upon the London audiences and Coram and Jerry soon found themselves in great demand. The duo began to headline at the principal theatres throughout the country and then made an extensive tour of the USA, where the original Jerry figure was destroyed during the great San Francisco earthquake in 1906. Fortunately Coram had several duplicates of Jerry's head to which he was continuously adding improvements, and eventually Jerry was capable of crying, winking, spitting, smoking, moving each eye independently and walking.

Coram and Jerry presenting their Whitehall scena in 1906.

Coram and Jerry who topped the bill with their military scena.

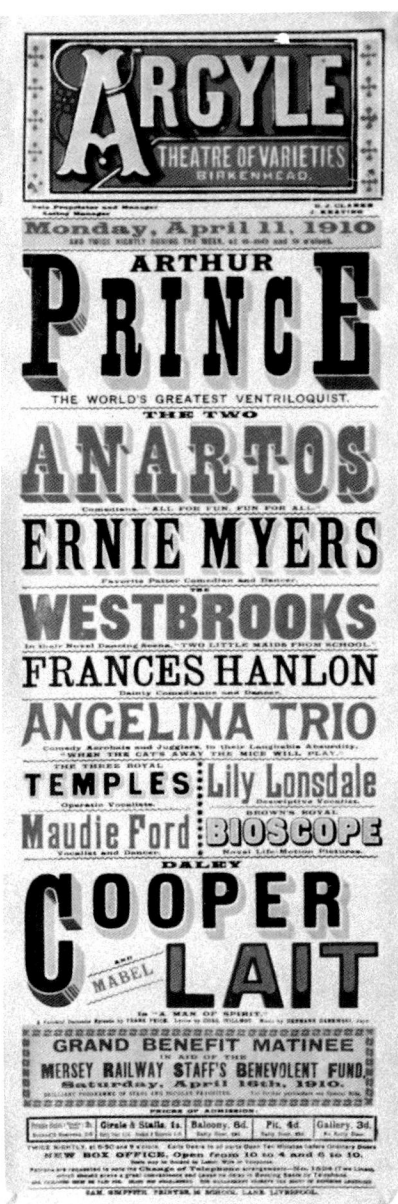

Coram improved not only the mechanics of his figure but also his act. He eventually adopted a military theme, appearing on stage as an officer with Jerry as Private Fisher. This military act greatly enhanced the popularity of his entertainment, and Jerry Fisher became the little man's hero. One of the highlights of his act was 'Jerry's Song',[5] which always prompted the audience to join him:

I'm Jerry Fisher, one of the old militia,
I'm Jerry Fisher in the morning
One of the rank and file
No wonder the ladies smile,
But I'm every inch a soldier.

Among the many successors of Fred Russell, none became more famous than Arthur Prince, who commanded one of the highest salaries in the business.

Prince was inspired as a teenager by the performances of Fred Russell and, with a burning desire to follow in his footsteps, he went to meet his idol after a show. Russell gave the seventeen-year-old Prince some advice on the rudiments of the art and later introduced him to a figure maker called LeMare. Prince commissioned the craftsman to make him a boy figure, whom he named Jim James, later known as Sailor Jim.[6]

Arthur Prince would often vary his nautical format by introducing new themes such as this Eastern scena in which his assistant played the part of an Arab Sheikh.

Facing: Arthur Prince and Jim in their famous nautical scena.

94

Johnson Clark and Hodge, his yokel character.

Facing: During the first world war the slogan 'Your Country Needs You' was reflected through the various military scenes presented by ventriloquial artists. Many of these postcards were sold to provide tobacco for the men at the front.

Prince eventually achieved his boyhood dream, becoming 'the world's greatest' and topped variety bills in every major city throughout the world. Like Coram, he adopted a military theme, presenting a nautical scene with elaborate sets and costumes with himself playing the admiral, his assistant as the first mate, and Jim the troublesome cabin boy.

The curtain rose to the strains of 'A Life on the Ocean Wave', revealing the forward deck of HMS *Seaworthy*, where Jim sat alone on a capstan. Then the first mate entered and warned Jim about the trouble he was in with the 'old man' who was shortly expected on deck.

Although Jim remained motionless throughout these opening moments, the figure's uncanny features led the audience to believe that he was listening to what was being said. Eventually Prince entered, immaculately dressed as the admiral. He acknowledged the audience's applause and then sat beside Jim to begin the give-and-take repartee.

In 1936, after touring the world with this nautical presentation, Prince decided to introduce a new scena called 'The Blue Diamond Club' centred on a life-sized figure name Monty. Set in Chicago's gangland era, the scena also featured Clifford Stanton as the cop and Prince's wife Julia Hartley as the 'moll'. Attired in tuxedos, Prince and Monty appeared as slightly inebriated toffs who inadvertently find themselves in the middle of a gangland feud.

Although this program received complimentary reviews for its staging and production, the new figure failed to have the same appeal as Jim, and after only a few performances Prince dropped the idea and reverted to his nautical scena.

Prince was a great showman and moved with the times, taking his art into every facet of the entertainment world. He appeared with Jim on radio and TV broadcasts, and in 1936 the duo were seen in a comic strip.[7]

In 1948, after almost fifty years in the business, the final curtain fell when the inseparable pair appeared at London's *Finsbury Park Empire*, where shortly after a performance, Arthur Prince died at the age of sixty-five.[8]

Other bill toppers were Tom Edwards[9], A. C. Astor[10] and Johnson Clark.[11] Prominent on the female side were Mabel Sinclair[12] and Maude Edwards, sister of Tom Edwards, who appeared in a riding scena with her stable boy Nobbler.[13]

These one-act sketches known as scenas, which were presented by ventriloquial artists at the time, required them to carry complete stage settings, enough for at least two changes of

ADKIN, The Motoring Ventriloquist.
In his successful scena,
"The Despatch Rider & The Boy Scouts"

program. Some were more elaborate than others. Johnson Clark's farmyard scena, centered on his yokel character Hodge, involved a farmyard stile, a wishing well and a telephone kiosk, as well as a painted backcloth depicting the English countryside. The assembling, staging and striking of these sets were performances in themselves, especially as most artists at the time relied upon public transport to take them from one venue to the next.

While two or three changes of program seemed adequate for most artists at the time, Leopoldo Fregoli had no fewer than sixty different acts, and travelled with 370 trunks containing 800 costumes, 1200 wigs, and thirty tons of scenery and props.

Born in Rome in 1867, Fregoli became the most celebrated Italian performer in this field of vocal jugglery. His one-man shows, seen by audiences throughout Europe, were elaborately staged productions in which he appeared as several different characters. To begin the show, Fregoli would introduce himself to the audience and sing a number of his own compositions. After the initial warm-up that gave Fregoli the 'feel' of the audience, the curtain rose to reveal a set depicting the dressing-room doors of the various artists. An actor playing the part of the stage manager explained to the audience that the show could not begin, as the artists had not yet arrived. Then Fregoli, dressed as a stagehand, offered to replace them and went through the first door quickly to reappear as the first artist, a French prima donna singing a soprano aria.

The show that followed displayed Fregoli's remarkable quick change artistry and diversified vocal talent as he appeared through the various doors, impersonating the missing artists who included a magician, singer, dancer, clown, juggler and ventriloquist. In his ventriloquial scena, he used five different characters. Through these, Fregoli would enact parodies of famous operas. When taking a bow he would rapidly change into the costumes of those he had impersonated.

This much loved artist died in Viareggio in 1936, where the epitaph on his tomb reads, 'Here Leopoldo Fregoli accomplished his last transformation'.[14]

In America, ventriloquist J. W. Cooper, who was known as 'The Black Napoleon of ventriloquism' presented a scena called 'Fun in a barber's shop' in which he appeared as a barber. He operated five characters. There was Jimmy, the newsboy, who stood between the two customers, Mr. Haskins seated in the chair and Mr. Jenkins waiting his turn. In the towel box (with only his head visible) was Sam the bootblack and next to him Miss Auto the manicurist, patiently waiting for her next customer.

Leopolo Fregoli, ventriloquist and quick-change artist.

Facing: Postcards, dating from 1905 to 1925, showing a variety of ventriloquial scenas. These presentations required artists to carry complete stage settings, enough for at least two program changes.

Cooper controlled the figures by means of fish lines attached to foot pedals concealed in the barber's chair.[15]

The Great Lester made his British debut at the *Hippodrome Theatre* in London in 1910. Born Maryan Czajkoski in Poland, Lester was one of the most celebrated names in American vaudeville, and has since become a cult figure among many ventriloquists in the USA. He would walk among the audience with his character Frank Byron Jr., and defy them to see any movement in his face or lips. He would also drink and smoke while his figure was talking. But his legendary reputation came from his distant voice display when he would call up heaven and hell on the telephone. The conversations at the other end were heard clearly, although at the same time they created the illusion of distance.[16]

In 1925, during a performance at a *Balaban and Katz Theatre* in Chicago, Lester's drinking feat was unexpectedly modified when straight whisky replaced the usual colored water in his decanter. The orchestra had switched drinks as a joke, trying to catch him off guard. When Lester innocently drank the liquid, not a muscle moved in his face, but the figure exploded in a storm of coughing. This piece of showmanship was so much appreciated by the

Facing: The Great Lester with Frank Byron Jr., his boy figure made by Theodore Mack in 1902. Lester, who was famous for his distant-voice technique on the telephone, has become a cult figure in America among exponents of the art.

Below: 'The Black Napoleon of Ventriloquism', John William Cooper, the first African-American ventriloquist, presenting his barber shop scene.

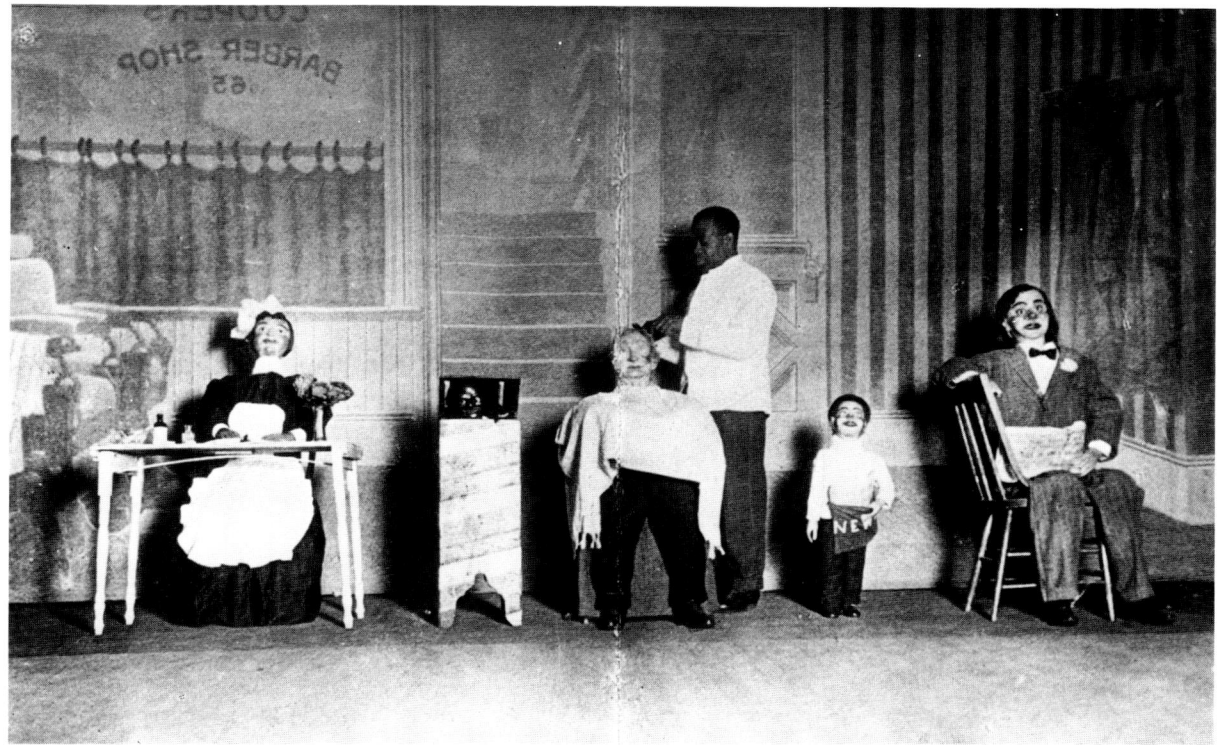

"THORA" VENTRILOQUIST

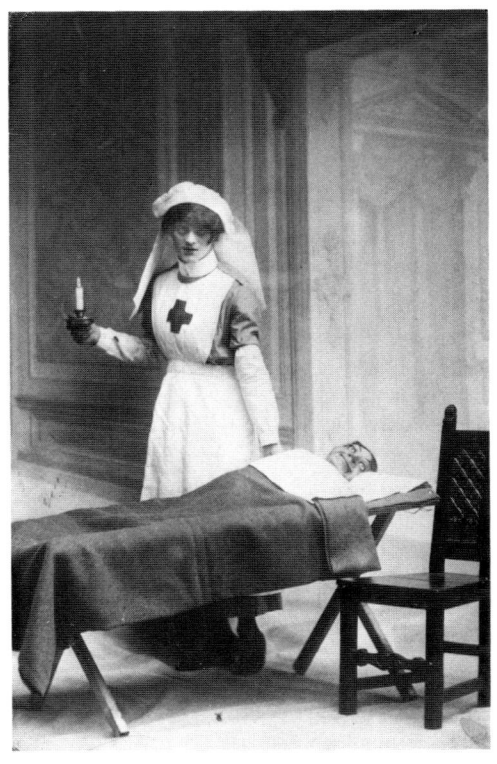

orchestra that they rose from their seats and applauded; the audience, sensing something unusual, joined in.

The 1920s saw the beginning of the end for variety entertainment because of the impact of moving pictures,[17] which were first introduced in theatres along with other supporting acts. Their popularity had increased to such a degree that many canopies outside the theatres read, 'Full-length pictures with added variety acts'. Some artists included bioscope showings in their program in an attempt to compensate for the increasing popularity of moving pictures.

Walter Lambert, who appeared as Lydia Dreams,[18] 'the ventriloquial and protean actor', opened his hospital scena with a film introduction showing a car accident. The scena continued in a hospital setting with Dreams playing a nurse and his figure the accident victim. Dreams, who began his theatrical career as a scene painter, always appeared on stage as a woman and while this novel presentation gained him recognition, it was his ability as an artist that brought him international fame. His painting 'Popularity', which hangs in the *Museum of London*, is a tribute to the golden variety era, depicting 230 variety artists.

Facing above: Maude Edwards with her stable boy and Mabel Sinclair with her coster figure. As female practitioners they were rare attractions and enjoyed the sovereignty of topping the bill.

Facing below: Female impersonators Thora (Hugh Thorn) and Lydia Dreams (Walter Lambert).

Below: Mrs. Clement De Lyon in her nursery tableau.

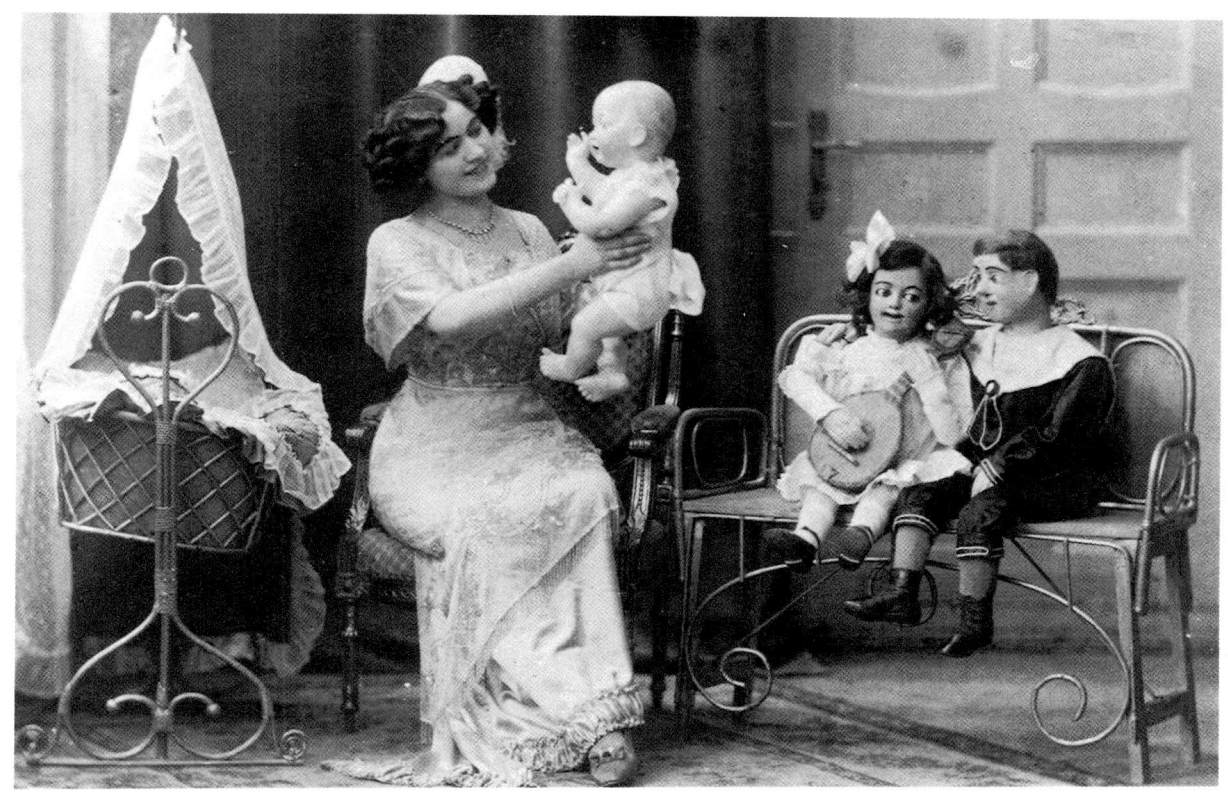

A poster of Lydia Dreams printed during the American tour in 1905.

Above: The painting 'Popularity' by Walter Lambert (Lydia Dreams). A masterful tribute to the British Music Hall era depicting portraits of 230 stage celebrities. The work measures thirteen feet by five and a half feet and was begun in 1901 and finished in 1903. It now hangs in the Museum of London. There are eight ventriloquists identified in the painting: Chirgwin, Lydia Dreams, Griff, Fred Russell, Capt. Slingsby, Lieut. Travis, Vento and Horace White (see key on page 220). Lambert died shortly before his eightieth birthday in 1950.

Right: Walter Lambert as Lydia Dreams, the character he portrayed in his ventriloquial performance.

Silent movies continued to increase in popularity over live variety and the final blow came in 1927 when sound was added to the flickering celluloid in a film called *The Jazz Singer,* starring Al Jolson. Hollywood followed this breakthrough with a series of musical films embracing the backstage lives of vaudeville artists. In 1929 ventriloquism was represented by this new medium in a film called *The Great Gabbo.*[19] This adaptation from a story by Ben Hecht portrayed the absorbing life of a ventriloquist whose sanity is threatened by his overwhelming egotism, while he projects his better side through his figure Otto. In his first 'talkie' Erich von Stroheim played Gabbo, proving himself as competent in sound as he had been on the silent screen and, in the tradition of Hollywood, the drama was lavishly dressed with spectacular sets, revue scenes and dance numbers.

In 1934 Lon Chaney portrayed the role of a ventriloquist, Professor Echo, in a film entitled *The Unholy Three.* This movie, first made as a silent feature in 1925,[20] also starring Chaney, was adapted from a story by C. A. Robbins. The trio referred to in the title are Professor Echo, a ventriloquist, Hercules, a strong man and Tweedledee, a midget. All are circus sideshow artists whose avocation is picking the pockets of the crowds who gather to see them. Eventually they abandon their circus careers altogether in search of bigger game, and open a shop which sells talking parrots. With ventriloquial aid from Professor Echo, who is disguised as the old lady of the shop, the birds can speak fluently until they are taken from the shop.

It is then that a further twist is added to the story. When a customer phones and complains that the purchased bird is silent, the old lady (Echo) together with her infant (Tweedledee) in the perambulator, visit the customer's house. While Echo and the customer examine the dumb creature, the midget nimbly leaves the perambulator and steals valuables throughout the house. In a later robbery, Hercules, the strong man, commits a murder which leads to the three's undoing.

In the original silent version, Chaney used a figure made by Theodore Mack, and the subsequent one an English figure by Herbert Brighton.

Facing: Eric von Stroheim as the Great Gabbo (1929) with his alter ego Otto that he eventually destroys.

Lon Chaney as Professor Echo in the 'Unholy Three,' which was first made as a silent movie in 1925 (right). The later 'all talking' version in 1934 (above) became Chaney's last screen appearance. He died shortly after the movie was completed.

Above: 'Magic,' starring Ann Margaret and Anthony Hopkins as Corky, the magician-ventriloquist whose animated dummy, Fats, manipulates his master into committing a series of terrifying murders (1978).

Facing: A poster of 'The Great Gabbo' showing the ventriloquist destroying the better side of his personality.

Left: 'Devil Doll,' starring Bryant Haliday as Vorelli, a ventriloquist who creates Hugo, a monster dummy he keeps in a cage (1963).

Below: The 1945 horror classic 'Dead of Night,' starring Sir Michael Redgrave as the deranged ventriloquist.

OFFICIAL COAST-TO-COAST PROGRAM GUIDE!

Radio Stars

LARGEST CIRCULATION OF ANY RADIO MAGAZINE

SEPTEMBER
10 CENTS

EDGAR BERGEN AND CHARLIE McCARTHY

THE GIRL WHO MIGHT HAVE OWNED HOLLYWOOD

7

Facing: Edgar Bergen and Charlie McCarthy. This celebrated duo became famous through their popular radio show in the nineteen thirties and forties.

VOICES IN THE AIR

In the same year that talking pictures were introduced, a young American ventriloquist made his debut on the English stage at London's *Holborn Theatre* in a sketch called 'The Operation'.[1] At the time the act went almost unnoticed by the critics, although it was well executed by the ventriloquist who played a concerned doctor trying to convince his small pug-nosed figure that his tonsils needed extracting. Few could tell that, almost a decade later, this small impish figure was to become as famous as any Hollywood star, his voice more familiar than the President's, and his name, besides becoming a household word, was to be introduced as a new synonym into the English language.[2]

Charlie McCarthy was undoubtedly the most illustrious piece of wood ever to grace a ventriloquist's knee. His creator, voice, and manipulator, Edgar John Bergen, was born in Chicago on February 16, 1903. Bergen experimented with magic, mind reading, and ventriloquism from his early youth. To a great extent he was inspired by *Hermann's Wizard's Annual*, which provided a crash course in the arts for twenty-five cents. In 1922 he sketched out Charlie McCarthy's features, which he modelled after an Irish schoolboy who sold newspapers near his school. He took the drawing to a woodcarver named Theodore Mack, who for $35 agreed to furnish a mouth-moving head. After purchasing

Below: Edgar Bergen, aged 18, with the original Charlie McCarthy.

the head, Bergen made a body, attached the two and christened the figure Charlie Mack, later adding the suffix.³

During his years at college Bergen's skills were employed by a local vaudeville theatre and shortly afterwards he graduated with a degree. He put aside his pre-medical studies and became a professional performer, doing four shows a day for $8 a week on the *Chautaugua Circuit*. Bergen fully used his various talents, and besides ventriloquism, incorporated magic and cartooning into his act. He also created another figure to accompany Charlie McCarthy, a genteel female named Laura.⁴

In 1927, Bergen went abroad and presented his 'operation scena', entertaining audiences throughout Europe. When he returned to America, he found the profession gloomily sounding the death knell of vaudeville. Determined not to sink with the ship, he decided to create a night club show which his agent at first tried to discourage as, up until this point, any kind of speaking act in a night club was practically unknown.

However, convinced that such an act would work, Bergen rewrote and polished his material to make it more suitable for the night club audience and eventually obtained a week's trial at the *Helen Morgan Club* in New York City.⁵

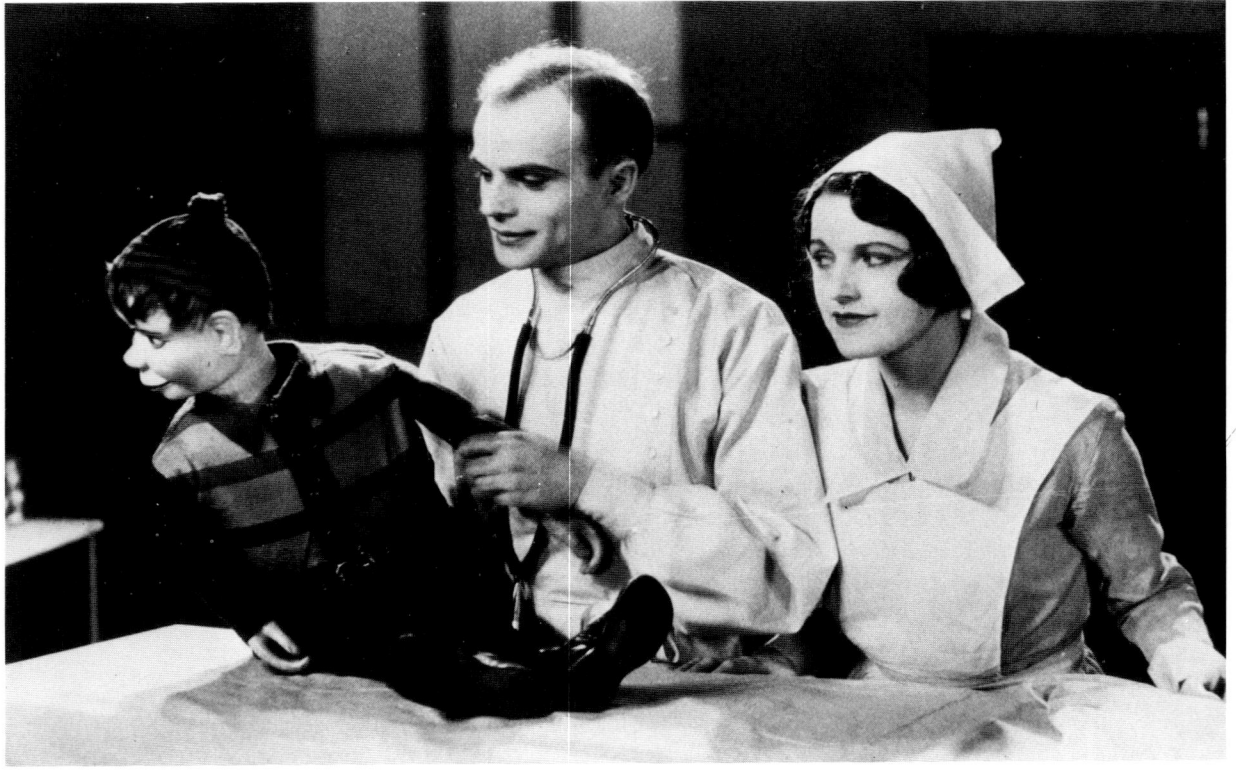

Below: The duo in 'The Operation' scena which they played on the American Vaudeville circuits and in theatres throughout Europe.

Above: Edgar Bergen in his early twenties, standing proudly beside a poster announcing his appearance on the Chautauqua circuit.

Left: Edgar Bergen at age 18 with Charlie McCarthy.

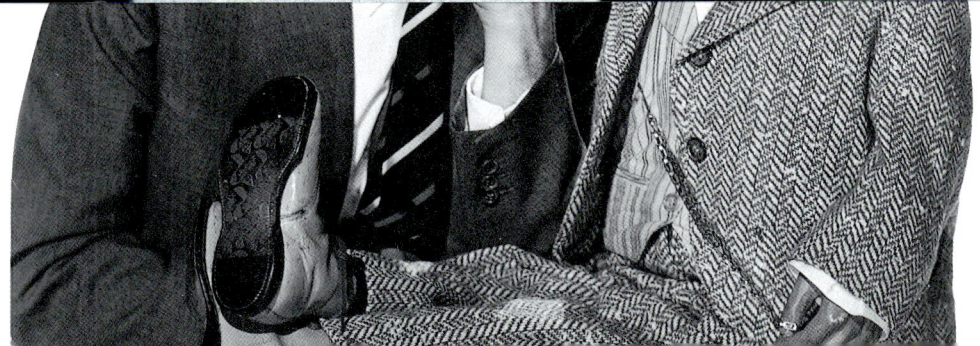

In the late forties Coca Cola sponsored the Bergen and McCarthy radio show (1949).

Facing: 'Charlie McCarthy Detective' (1939).

Bergen's keen sense of showmanship maintained this illusion off stage as well as on. Charlie was heard shouting for release as Bergen took him from his velvet-lined case. During rehearsals Charlie would always insist upon reading the scripts, and visitors to Bergen's home were amused to find that Charlie had his own room, complete with writing desk, bed and wardrobe, full of specially tailored suits for his various roles. On the writing desk a note, which Bergen claimed Charlie had scribbled, read, 'Sorry Charlie could not attend school today. He had lary larn [crossed out]. He had to visit his sick grandmother'.[11]

The popularity of Charlie McCarthy was lucratively exploited in a mass of commercially produced items, including comic books, pea shooters, bubble gum, sweatshirts and a variety of toys and gadgets, as well as Charlie McCarthy dolls.

Eventually, the demand to see Charlie as well as hear him resulted in a movie contract.[12] The first Bergen-McCarthy feature was *A Letter of Introduction* (1938), in which Bergen played an out-of-work ventriloquist. Although this was their first full-length picture, the duo were no newcomers to the cinema. Before their radio success, they had made a series of shorts for Vitaphone. Undoubtedly their most popular feature film was *You Can't Cheat an Honest Man* (1939) which co-starred Charlie's old rival, W.C. Fields, and the Fields and McCarthy feud was resumed on celluloid.

In America, ventriloquism itself underwent a renaissance during this period, and figure makers throughout the USA found that their skills were in demand once again. Veteran vaudevillians

old Brough to take, but, realizing that he had learned only the basic technique of his craft, he decided to start again. In the following weeks he began to develop an entirely new act, experimenting with different voices until he arrived at the thin treble of a fourteen-year-old boy, a voice that eventually became familiar to millions. The next important step was to create a figure to fit the voice, and Brough sketched out a design which he took to master craftsman Len Insull. He made up three prototypes and after Brough had chosen one, the new figure was made up for a total cost of £250.[22]

After naming the dummy Archie Andrews, Peter Brough turned his energies to the most popular medium of the time, radio. His first broadcast was in 1943, on a top variety program called *Music Hall*. A whole year elapsed before his next radio appearance on a program called *Navy Mixture*. It resulted in a forty-six-week run.[23]

At the time, Brough was extremely impressed by the Bergen and McCarthy broadcasts which were heard in Britain via the overseas forces network. He decided to pursue a similar idea for British radio and approached the BBC with the idea of building a show around Archie. Although the BBC turned down Brough's original idea for the *Archie Andrews Show*, they accepted the second proposal, *Two's a Crowd*,[24] which had as well as the duo, impersonator Peter Cavanagh, 'the voice of them all', as the sole

Some of the many commercially-produced items resulting from Peter Brough's creation, Archie Andrews.

Young Archie won't "pipe down"!

Script conference for 'Educating Archie.' Left to right: Julie Andrews, Robert Moreton, Archie Andrews, Hattie Jacques, Peter Brough, Max Bygraves and Roy Speer.

luggage ticket and a note that read, 'You will find Archie at King's Cross'. Brough hurried down to King's Cross Station and found his suitcase with Archie intact but, as Brough put it, 'suffering from a slight loss of memory as to exactly what had happened'. The writer of the letter remained a mystery, and Brough wrote many years later, 'Who was he, the original thief or some soft-hearted accomplice?'[27]

In 1953, the *Daily Mail* announced that *Educating Archie* had again been voted the best radio program, and won its Silver Mike for the second time.[28] During its run it had had various changes, adding Tony Hancock, Beryl Reid and Harry Secombe to its cast. There were also special guest stars, including Edgar Bergen. *Educating Archie* was last heard in 1958 and Peter Brough's success was climaxed when Madame Tussaud's waxworks made effigies of him and his famous figure for their gallery of radio stars.

It has often been stated that ventriloquism became farcical on radio because the ventriloquist was unseen, but it must be remembered that ventriloquism is essentially a vocal, not a visual illusion. The art of the ventriloquist is to create not only other voices, but more importantly, other personalities. To convincingly convey to the audience the reality of these imaginary characters through skilful voice changes, banter and comic timing.

In many ways radio was a more difficult arena than the stage presentation of the art where the ventriloquist is *visually* aided by the mouth-moving figure. Radio relied solely upon the ears of its audience. In this medium a different technique was required from the stage presentation of the art. It was necessary for the ventriloquist to be punctilious and articulate so the ventriloquial voices could be heard clearly. For this, both Bergen and Brough dispensed with lip control, realizing the importance that their character voices register clearly upon the ears of the millions who were listening.

Nevertheless, the radio success of Edgar Bergen and Peter Brough clearly indicated they were masters of their art, and by adapting ventriloquism to radio, they not only brought it to a place of prominence but also insured its popularity which could otherwise have faded.

Below: Peter Brough and Archie Andrews during a broadcast of the B.B.C. radio show 'Educating Archie.'

8

Facing: Two wooden figures made by Frank Marshall in the nineteen twenties. Both have the drop jaw movement and moving-winking eyes. The walking figure, on the right, measures 5 feet tall and is capable of spitting and crying.

SPEAKING DOLLS

The ventriloquial figure, commonly known as a dummy or doll, has not only become synonymous with the art, but has emerged as a focal point of the practice. Today, it is rare to witness a ventriloquial performance that does not include some form of figure, yet it is a relatively new addition to ventriloquial performances. Before its introduction, the ventriloquist's 'familiar' was invisible, its physical form perceived only through the audience's imagination. However, by the adoption of the ventriloquial figure, the art was given a new dimension, which in turn increased its popularity.

Over the years, figures have been fashioned from almost every kind of material and made to represent a host of different characters, animal and human, animate and inanimate. Their internal operations have also been varied, with many containing scores of complicated movements which have mirrored nature's operations, enabling them to move their limbs, eyes, eyebrows, ears, noses and mouths—to stand, sit, talk, cry, laugh, smoke, spit and sleep.

In spite of the ingenuity of internal mechanism, the illusion of the talking figure relies upon the basic movement of the mouth which, when moved in conjunction with the ventriloquial voice, gives the appearance of speaking.

Below: Australian ventriloquist Ron Blaskett and Gerry Gee, made by Frank Marshall for the opening of Melbourne television in 1957. The duo continued to star in their own show for more than twenty years, and Gerry's fan club had over 200,000 members.

It was this simple but effective movement which the Baron Von Mengen installed into the small doll during his performances in Vienna. In a letter to the Abbe de la Chapelle dated February 17, 1770, he gave a detailed description of the figure and its operation, saying, 'The doll is nothing but a plain wooden figure, fitted with a nutcracker mouth, quite wide and toothless. On both sides of the mouth, hidden in the folds of the skin, is the opening of the lower half of the mouth which can be made to open by means of a device clear through the middle of the neck. Both eyes are open and enamelled and polished to glow in a natural manner. Its size is just that of a big man's hand from head to body. The head is covered with a Turkish turban. The rest of the body is limbless—no arms, no feet, and clad only with a cloak'.[1]

To operate the doll, the Baron held it in his left hand under the

Below: Fred Russell's patent for 'Improvements in Ventriloquial Apparatus' (1907).

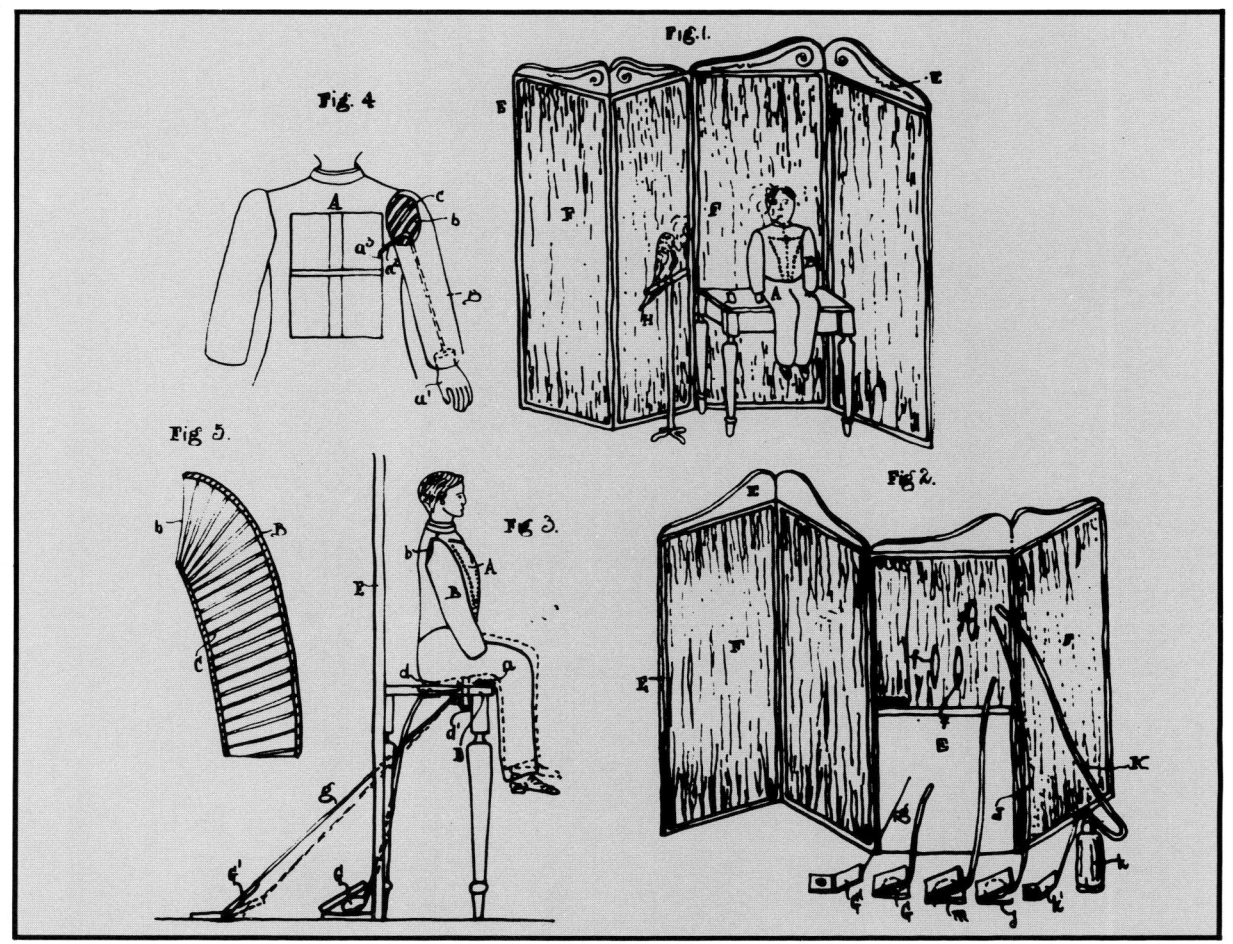

cloak which hid the mechanism controlling the mouth movements. Then, through his skilful manipulation and ventriloquy, 'the voice seemed to come out of the mouth of the doll as if it were really alive'. The Baron said that this required a great deal of attention, 'for, if the movement of the mouth did not absolutely conform with the natural articulation of vowels and words, the illusion would vanish'.

The following is an extract from the Baron's performance with his mouth-moving figure at the Bayreuth court in 1757.

Baron: Hello, girlie. I heard bad things about you.

Doll: Slander is easy, sir. Don't leave the straight path. It's easy to enter.

Baron: You're a little coquette. You stir up men, like it or not.

Doll: Sir, when one has a grain of beauty, she is exposed to envy and persecution.

Baron: Girlie, you do some tall reasoning.

Doll: Sir, it is not permitted always to attach oneself to someone else, but one is always allowed to defend oneself.[2]

Below: British figure maker Geoff Felix, who, following in the footsteps of his mentor Len Insull, prefers to use traditional methods and materials to produce his fine creations.

Apart from the human and animal caricatures, ventriloquists have employed, over the years, many novelty items such as this Jack-in-the-box featured by Claude Chandler.

Below: Other novelties include Handbag Harry, unfolding from a handbag into a figure with moving mouth and eyes; a Toby jug with smiling mouth and eye movements, made by Len Insull; a mouth-moving walking cane by D'Albert and an Insull pocket figure with balance eyes and pneumatically-operated mouth. (All are composite.)

Although the mouth-moving figure was introduced in the eighteenth century, it was almost a hundred years before it became a fashionable part of the ventriloquial repertoire. Even then many prominent exponents such as Love and Maccabe preferred their 'familiars' to remain invisible. However, during the early days of music hall, 'speaking dolls' as they were called, became increasingly popular and soon were the accepted accompaniment of the ventriloquist. At first, many performers used only mouth-moving heads, but because of their novelty, the crudeness of these early figures was overlooked. As the usage of the automaton increased, so did the workmanship that went into making them, and figures became more refined.

When the ventriloquist surrounded himself with a 'row' or family of automata, a variety of characters emerged, the most popular being the old man and woman. Black figures were also a great favorite derived from the popular minstrel entertainment.

Apart from the human caricatures, there were many other kinds of ingenious automata such as mouth-moving Toby jugs, clocks, and head-mounted walking canes, plus a variety of animal characters. At the turn of the century, when the single figure method became the vogue, duos such as Fred Russell and Coster Joe, Arthur Prince and Jim and Coram and Jerry popularized the 'cheeky boy' character which emerged, and for the most part this has remained the familiar accompaniment of the ventriloquist.

Many ventriloquists, such as Harry Vento, preferred to fashion and design their own figures. Vento made a series of ingenious automata which he not only used himself, but supplied to his fellow professionals.[3]

In 1893 Frank Millis patented a design for operating figures pneumatically, controlling the different hinged parts[4] by expelling air into a series of bladders which in turn activated the various movements. Some years later Fred Russell also registered a patent for 'improvements in ventriloquial apparatus'.[5] They enabled a figure to light up a cigarette prior to the ventriloquist's entrance by means of a concealed assistant who substituted his own arm in place of the figure's.

At the time, when electricity was still a novelty, Walter Cole installed a bulb into the nose of his old man figure. When it lit up the old man would shout, 'Blow it out, Cole', which evoked laughter and applause from the audience. Despite such innovations, ventriloquial figures are traditionally operated by a simple spring mechanism attached to strings which, when pulled, initiate the various movements.

Below: A leprechaun character handcarved from basswood by America's master figure maker Tim Sëlberg. Sëlberg's combination of technical skill and artistic talent have made him a virtuoso of his art.

A Mack head, made of wood, with moving jaw and eyes.

The promotion of the character creation, rather than the technique of the artist, increased the popularity of the art and at the same time created a greater demand for figures. Several suppliers of theatrical apparatus began producing a wide selection for both the amateur and the professional performer. In France, Julian Petee began producing ventriloquial figures in 1845 and continued this small business after he emigrated to America at the turn of the century. His son, Revello Petee, eventually succeeded him and was also responsible for establishing the first circular devoted entirely to ventriloquism, called *Double Talk* (1937-1939).[6]

Figure makers were usually classed as theatrical properties suppliers, and a prominent firm in England was Alfred Lemare and Sons, who established their business in 1861. Lemare made a variety of properties for the theatre but specialized in ventriloquial and magical apparatus. Through the window of their small shop in Manchester, England, could be seen a colorful display of knee figures, including clowns, costers, sailors and boy and girl characters. Their catalogue listed the variety available, with the lure, 'These figures are well designed and in good proportion'. Besides the popular knee figures, Lemare and Sons made the talking hand, 'a nicely dressed figure whose head is a glove into which the hand is placed. Price 2s 6d'.

There were also novelty items such as 'Dancing Figure, 32 inches high on a pedestal with black curtain. The figure is worked by one string and can be operated from any distance and dances in a most artistic way. Price £3'. Lemare and Sons, who supplied figures for over seventy years, prided themselves in making properties for some of the top ventriloquial performers, including Fred Russell and Arthur Prince.[7]

Another father and son team were Theodore and Charles Mack of Chicago, who were first introduced to figure making by Harry (The Great) Lester. After his own figure was stolen, Lester found the wood carvers' name in the telephone directory and asked them to make him a replacement. Thus began the Macks' career as figure makers; they were primarily ornate wood carvers doing architectural and cabinet work. Their reputation grew and they eventually printed a catalogue of their work.

In 1922, seventeen-year-old Edgar Bergen went to the Macks' shop on the north side of Chicago and asked the craftsmen to carve out a head, following the sketch he had made. However, the cost of this custom-made figure proved too great for the young ventriloquist's pocket and he settled for a stock figure instead. In an attempt to comply with some individuality, the Macks agreed to make a slight alteration to the nose and, for a cost of $35, Bergen had Charlie McCarthy.

An employee at the Mack shop was Frank Marzalkiewicz, who had also been introduced to the business by Harry Lester. Lester, who was then his neighbor, suggested wood carving as a form of rehabilitation as Marzalkiewicz suffered from polio. In 1913, Lester introduced the teenager to the Macks who employed him as an apprentice. After working there for some years he changed his name to Frank Marshall, eventually bought out the business from the Macks, and went on to become America's most celebrated figure maker. Besides the ventriloquial properties, among which were Danny O'Day and Jerry Mahoney, Marshall produced hand puppets, marionettes and Punch and Judy sets. He died in 1969.[8]

The reputation of Mack and Marshall set a trend in North America which favored wooden carved figures. In this they differed from their fellow-craftsmen in Europe, who preferred paper composite figures. In consequence, many of the old vaudeville gags referring to the figure's woodiness are still heard today, although modern materials such as fiberglass and plastics are in use.

Below: Frank Marshall carving a head from basswood. Marshall became America's most renowned figure maker, and his creations have shared the spotlight with many of the world's top ventriloquists.

The McElroy brothers in their workshop in 1940 with their umpire automaton.

Below: The McElroy brothers admiring their creation "Dudley."

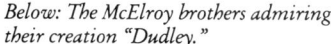

Above: Dennis Alwood and Dudley, made by the McElroy Brothers in 1965. Alwood was the voice and animator of Fats in the movie 'Magic' and also became the authorized voice of Charlie McCarthy after Edgar Bergen's death.

Facing: A tribute to the McElroy Brothers by Bill Nelson. George and Glenn McElroy were considered the most innovative makers of ventriloquial figures.[9] What started out as a hobby eventually became a full time profession, and in the thirties and forties they supplied custom made figures to some of the top names in the business, including Bob Neller and Rudy Vallee.

Facing: The inner workings of the figure. Illustration by Bill Nelson.

Below: A selection of professional figures offered in 1931.

COSTER BILL

A really good figure with a very comical expression. Well made, with mouth and eye movements.

Price ... **55/-**

Pearl Button Costume, 10/- extra.

BOY SCOUT

An excellent knee figure —well dressed, and a real laughter provoking expression.

Price **55/-**
Superior Quality **65/-**

"SOLOMON SLOW"
The Messenger

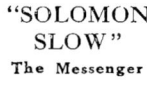

A very natural figure with a really funny head. Lends itself to a good style of dialogue.

Price ... **55/-**
Superior Quality **65/-**

In England at the turn of the century, Edwin Simms began producing ventriloquial figures from his London studio under the pseudonym A. Quisto. Quisto was considered an eccentric recluse, and eventually moved his business to a caravan on the Devon coast. It was there that he died as the result of a fall from a ladder while attempting to paint the outside of his caravan during a storm in the middle of the night.[10]

Other prominent English makers were Herbert Brighton, D'Albert and Leonard Insull. Born in 1893, Insull began his career in the theatre as a comedy illusionist appearing under the name of Hinsle. For twenty years he performed in theatres around the world assisted by his wife, who appeared as Miss Gertie Rees.

Shortly after World War I, Leonard Insull began a stage property business in Wolverhampton. It was there that Coram challenged him with the words, 'I bet you couldn't make me a dummy'. Insull could and did, eventually becoming the most sought after British maker of ventriloquial properties.[11]

After successfully making the first figure for Coram, he began to experiment and made a series of 'cheeky boy' heads to which he fitted complicated movements that enabled their faces to become fully animated. His work, which is often distinguishable by the fine leather mouth movement and delicately painted face, was supplied to artists around the world. Among his famous creations were Ray Alan's Lord Charles and Peter Brough's Archie Andrews. Equally creative was his son Leonard Insull Jr., who assisted his father and was responsible for creating many of the novelty items, including the Toby jug and the pneumatically operated pocket figure. Insull outlived his son by seventeen years and continued to produce ventriloquial properties until his death in 1974 at the age of eighty-one.

Although the operation and design of the ventriloquial figure continued to improve, its individual popularity still depends upon the manipulative and ventriloquial skill of the artist behind it, infusing the character with an individual voice and personality. This schizophrenic ability, which ventriloquists develop by talking to themselves, has often been the subject of controversy and provides an intriguing vehicle for the dramatist and fiction writer.

Ventriloquists, in order to project the illusion of their figure's reality, enact the belief that they are real. Many artists have opened up bank accounts for their figures, listed their names in telephone directories, and even entered them as candidates in election campaigns.

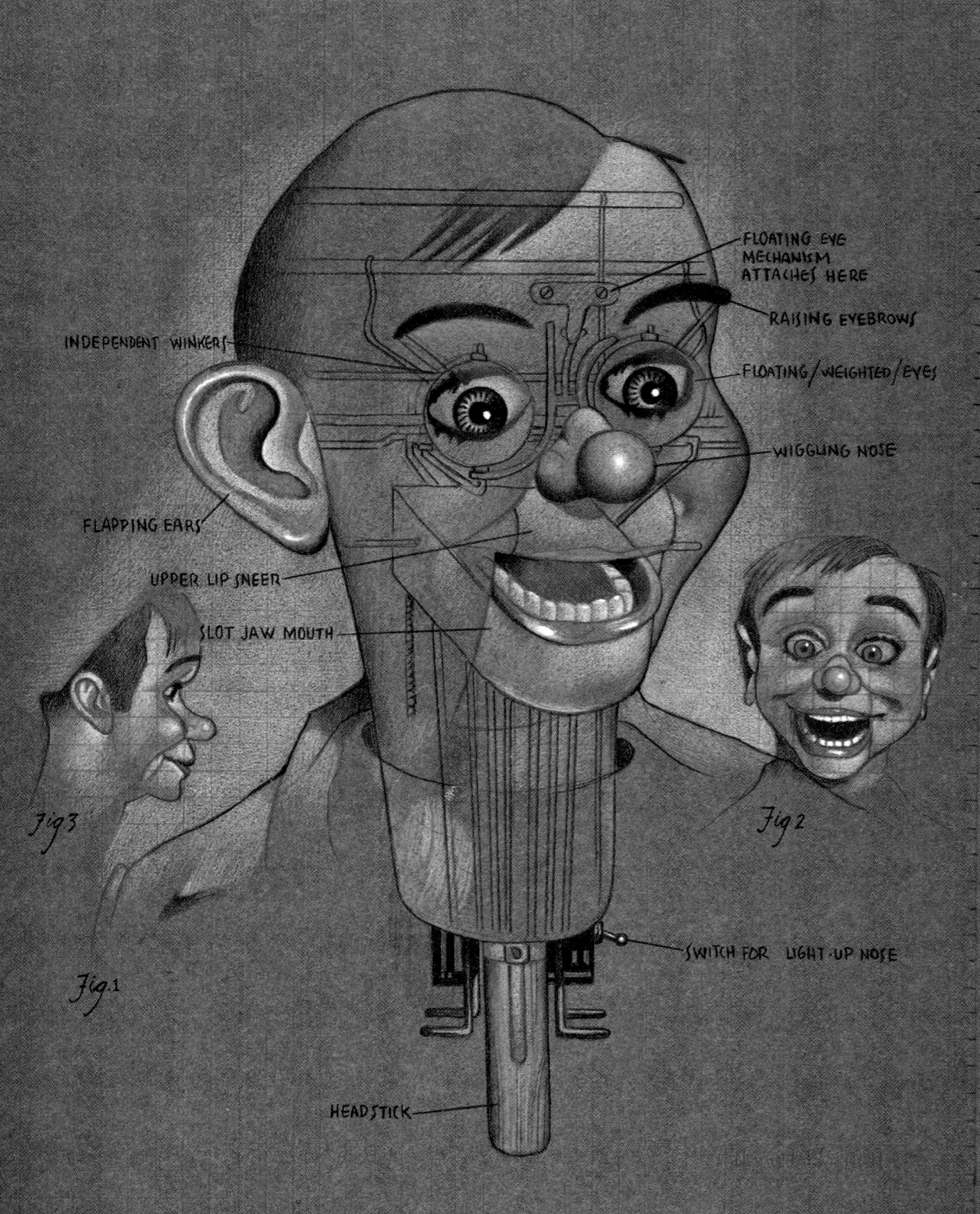

Mouth.

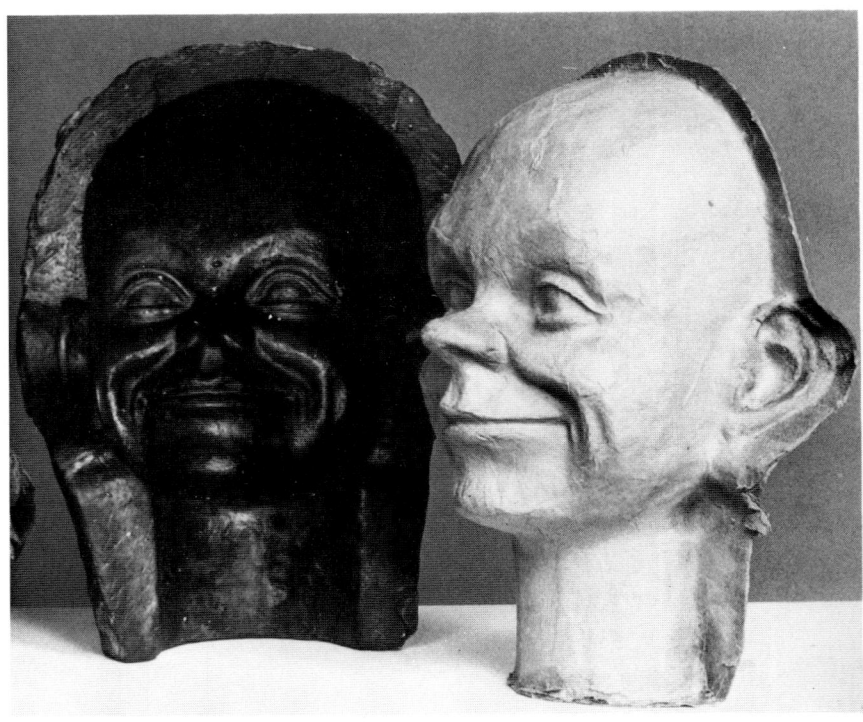

Smile.

The Insull moulds for making composite figures. Specially treated paper is pressed into the mould to form the shell. When it is dry the various movements are added. Holes for the eyes and mouth animation are cut out and, as an alternative to the drop jaw, fine leather is used to simulate the mouth movement.

Eyes.

Eyebrows.

Winking.

Ears.

Although this showmanship is part of the business of the entertainment world, the ventriloquist's involvement in this façade is often found suspended between illusion and reality. During an engagement in Las Vegas, ventriloquist Jimmy Nelson once waited for his figure Danny O'Day to sing the last line of their closing song. The song was performed by Nelson in a rapid exchange of three different voices, but when it came to the final line no sound issued from the figure. Nelson had forgotten for that second that *he* was providing the voice, and waited for the character to finish the song.[12] This strange separation of personality was underlined by Tony Hancock, who played the tutor opposite Archie Andrews in *Educating Archie*. Hancock always insisted that Archie be there, even during rehearsals. 'I must have Archie alive', he said.[13]

While the ventriloquist's dummy merely embodies the extension or expression of the ventriloquist's own personality, it is evident that many artists develop a certain attachment to their figures. The care and attention that Herbert Dexter gave to his figure Charlie proved precarious to his matrimonial state and resulted in a divorce suit in which his wife named the mechanical figure as co-respondent.[14]

At first, the court was amused when blues singer Sally Osman described how her ventriloquist husband spent more time talking to his 'miserable dummy' than to her. Her case became more

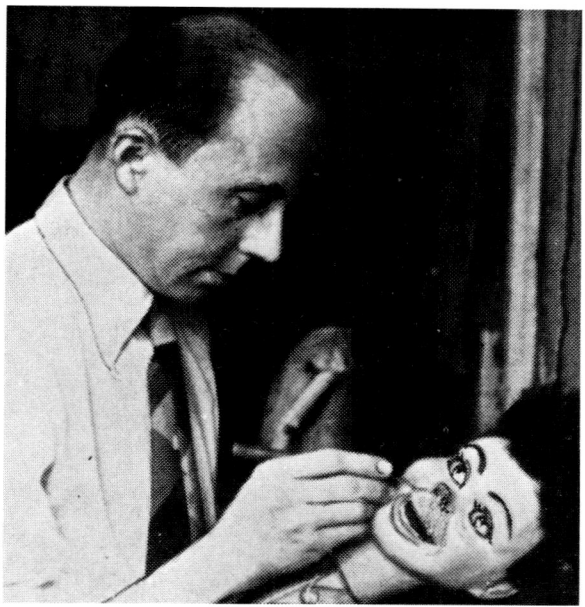

Below: Two generations of ventriloquial figure-makers, Len Insull Jr. (left), and Len Insull Snr. with his wife, Gertie.

Facing: Herbert Dexter with his wife, Sally Osman, and Charlie, his animated partner who was named as correspondent in their divorce suit.

Below: Jimmy Nelson with Danny O'Day and Farfel. Nelson, one of the greatest rapid voice change technicians, has remained in the spotlight through the widely syndicated commercial for Nestles.

convincing, however, as she revealed the facts about her two-year-old marriage to the Australian ventriloquist. It appeared that when she first married Dexter in 1932, Charlie was on his best behavior, and she voiced no objection to him being taken along on their honeymoon as some of the nicest things her husband ever said to her came through the lips of the dummy.

But, things began to change when she and her husband developed a new stage act together. She became sadly disillusioned when she found herself the target of ridicule as Charlie interrupted her singing with cruel ad libs. After her number, the audience's appreciation of her singing was quickly dispelled; Charlie would cut in with a ruinous wisecrack before they could applaud.

She tried to make her husband change the act so that she could sing without any interruptions from Charlie, but he refused to listen. She also accused the duo of physical cruelty, telling the court how she constantly received on-stage blows from the mechanical figure, which left her with severe bruises. One night in particular, Charlie had hit her so hard between the shoulder blades that he knocked the wind out of her. Had her husband

done this, he would have received a hostile reaction from the audience; instead, they laughed and applauded. The fully-automatic Charlie had been developed by Dexter in Germany with the aid of the best toymakers.

Sally Osman further testified that their social life was also ruined because Dexter would insist upon taking her mechanical rival everywhere they went and would spend more time talking with Charlie than with her. The court heard how the singer's mental state was being affected by this strange triangle she was involved in. She said, 'I got to hate Charlie so deeply that homicidal thoughts began to haunt my mind. Sometimes when I had Charlie alone and helpless, I fear that I would have thrown him out of the window, had I been able to unlock the coffin-like trunk in which he was kept'.

She added, 'When we had company, Charlie's behavior was even more outrageous. One time, I was singing for friends in our apartment the song, 'I'm Alone Because I Love You'. Charlie interrupted with, 'Well, if loving him keeps you alone, I hope

W.S. Berger at the Vent Haven Museum in Kentucky, with some of his collection of figures.

you never stop'.

Herbert Dexter never contested the case and his wife was granted a divorce. In summing up, Judge Allegretti asked the plaintiff why she had not requested alimony. She said, 'I wouldn't be able to collect it anyway; he spends all his money on Charlie'.

When a ventriloquist dies, the figure, if not left to the ravages of woodworm, is often passed on to another entertainer, as was Arthur Worsley's Charlie Brown, who was working the halls long before Worsley was born. If it is a famous figure it could find its last resting-place in a museum, like Coster Joe, who keeps a silent vigil at the famous *Water Rats Club* in London, where his master was thrice king. Coram's Jerry Fisher is also carefully preserved at the Museum of London and is occasionally displayed during special theatrical exhibitions.

During the zenith of his fame Edgar Bergen, fearing that Charlie McCarthy would be forgotten in the event of his death, drew up a will that bequeathed Charlie the sum of ten thousand dollars. Bergen appointed the *America Actors Guild* as trustees

Part of the exhibit at the Museum Der Bauchrednerkunst (Museum of Ventriloquism) in Degersheim, Switzerland, that was designed and built by the author in 1985.

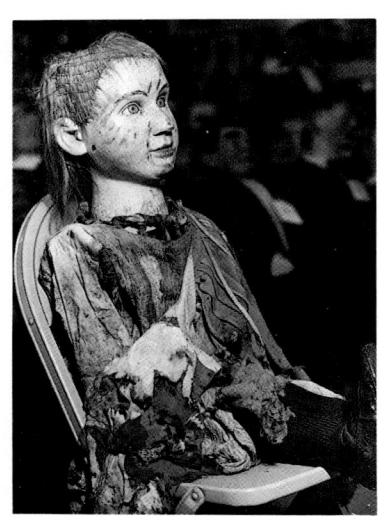

In the Vent Haven Museum, this salt crusted figure was one of the survivors of a shipwreck that took its master's life off the coast of Mexico in 1908.

who were requested to appoint qualified ventriloquists to keep Charlie working and therefore remain in the public eye. However, the eventual enormity of Charlie McCarthy's fame overrode this original will and shortly before his death, Bergen donated the original figure to the Smithsonian Institute where he is now on permanent display.[15]

For ventriloquist Arthur Prince the final curtain did not sever him from the embodiment of his alter ego. The famous duo known as 'Arthur Prince and Jim' were inseparable, even, it seems, after death. For when Arthur Prince died in 1948, Jim, his lifelong companion, was buried in the same grave as his master.[16]

In America, a retired ventriloquial figure may find itself spending the remainder of its days at a 'home' for dummies called Vent Haven. Devoted entirely to ventriloquism, the Vent Haven Museum, Inc. houses hundreds of figures, playbills, photographs, books, recordings, and memorabilia pertaining to the ventriloquial art. Its founder was William Shakespeare Berger, the son of a German actor who, after his retirement from the business world, began collecting ventriloquiana and eventually amassed over 500 figures and a library of recorded and printed matter.[17]

Shortly after he began accumulating his collection, Berger became the president of the International Brotherhood of Ventriloquists, a fraternity formed exclusively for exponents of the practice. Its official publication, *The Oracle*[18] (formerly the *Grapevine News*),[19] was circulated to members in nearly thirty countries and contained articles, news and advice concerning the art. In 1963, after a lapse of three years, the IBV was succeeded by the International Ventriloquists' Association whose organizers, Walter and Gregory Berlin, also published its official organ, *Ventogram*.[20] Berger wrote regular column 'flashes' for all three publications until shortly before his death in 1970.

Berger's collection is now housed at his former home in Fort Mitchell, Kentucky, where it has been incorporated into a trust to preserve it as a permanent institution, open to the public and devoted to furthering the ventriloquial art. Inside the three small buildings that contain the collection, the walls are covered with photographs, playbills and paintings of ventriloquists past and present, and hundreds of figures sit or stand in silent rows. Most of these were purchased by Berger himself, while others were donated or willed by ventriloquists who preferred their retired partners to be silently preserved in this memorial to double talk.

Many figures were owned by former stars, such as Frank Byron Jr., who belonged to the Great Lester. A special section devoted to Lester shows various props, including his telephone, fitted with a mirror so that Lester could check his lip movements. Among other fascinating acquisitions is a set of figures which belonged to the American ventriloquist W.H. Wood, who performed around 1900.[21] This pathetic family of salt-encrusted figures were the only survivors of a shipwreck which took their master's life in the Gulf of Mexico in 1908. Although the collection largely pertains to the American ventriloquists, it has a number of acquisitions from famous international artists such as Lydia Dreams, Jules Vernon, Coram, Eric Everty and many more.

In Europe, the collaboration between the author and Swiss entrepreneur Retonio Breitenmoser resulted in the establishment of Europe's first ventriloquial museum in 1985. Set in the picturesque Canton of St. Gallen in Eastern Switzerland, the *Museum Der Bauchrednerkunst*[22] graphically exhibits the history of ventriloquism from ancient times to the present day. Like its American counterpart, it houses hundreds of figures and acquisitions pertaining to the art. Of particular interest is the abundant display of printed matter—from ancient theological treatises to the Edwardian postcard collection. There is also a small movie theatre where a clip from the movie *Magic* is concluded with the startling appearance of its star 'Fats.' Fully animated, Fats greets his guests by reciting the sinister poem from the movie.

In recent years there has been a diversion from the lifelike caricature towards the more abstractly featured one, but the ventriloquial figure, whether elaborately carved or a simple caricature made of cloth, remains the focal point of a performance.

Its present position was perhaps foreseen by Frederick Maccabe in 1875 who, after witnessing a performance by E.D. Davies with his two knee figures 'Tommy and Joe', wrote, 'May he find many imitators, so that when, in the course of time, he must shuffle off this mortal coil, the little fairy dolls will live on to make millions merry among generations unborn'.[23]

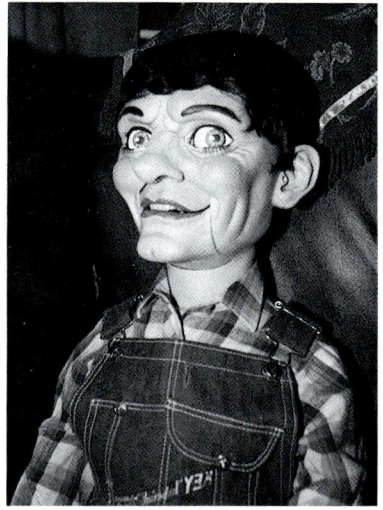

At the 'Museum of Ventriloquism' in Switzerland, 'Fats,' the sinister dummy from the movie 'Magic', waits for the unsuspecting visitor to trigger his automated mechanism which brings him to life.

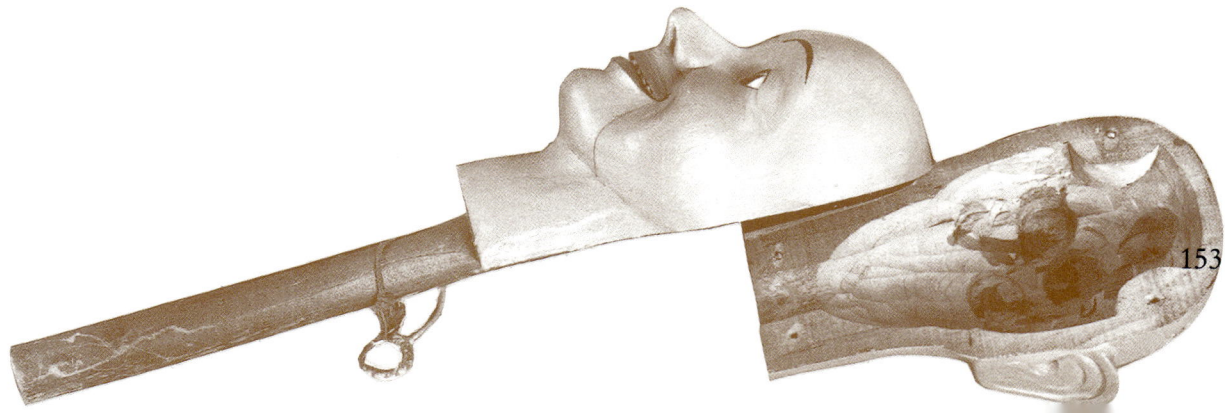

Farewell to ARTHUR

Especially written for
"JIM"

To whom words of his own do not come easily.
—By RICHARD GOOLDEN.

I quickened at his touch, he gave me breath.
His magic finger moved my Puppet lips,
Now he is gone the "Floats" are dimmed by death,
And side by side we lie in mute eclipse.

In him alone, I moved and breathed and spoke,
You who remain, may <u>Voice</u> your sorrowing love,
No words, Alas! can humble "<u>Jim</u>" evoke
To mourn the passing of his pal "The Guv."

Yet, though in silence I must "Go below,"
And leave this "Life Upon The Ocean Wave,"
There Is a glory on me as I go,
Oh! lucky "Jim" to share a Prince's grave.

from JULIE PRINCE

ARTHUR PRINCE
&
JIM
DIED 14TH APRIL 1948

JULIE PRINCE
DIED 14TH SEPT. 1949

The grave of Arthur Prince and Jim. When the famous duo were laid to rest in a London cemetery, this poem by Richard Goolden was sent to friends and relatives of the ventriloquist. His widow, Julie Prince, died one year later and was buried in the same grave.

When the single knee figure became the vogue, it increased the popularity of the art and ventriloquists appeared on almost every variety bill as well as in concerts and at seaside resorts. At that time, picture postcards were the advertising hand-outs for these artists. The following pages show a selection of postcards from the author's collection.

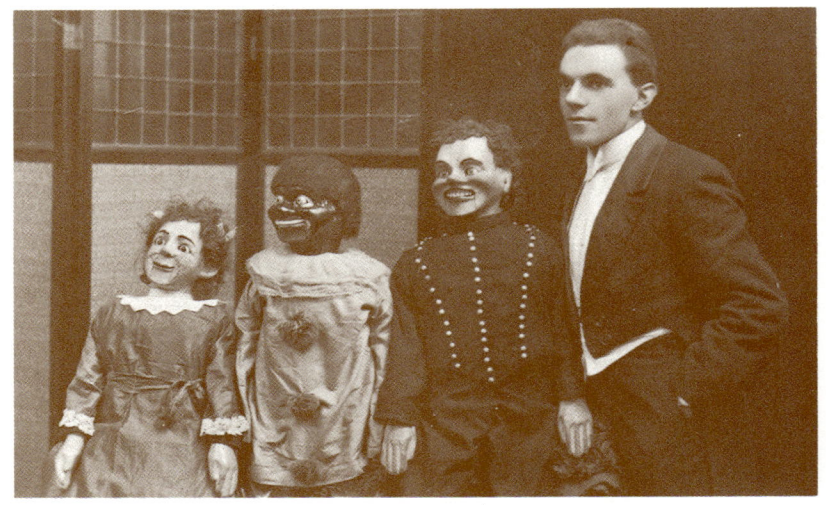

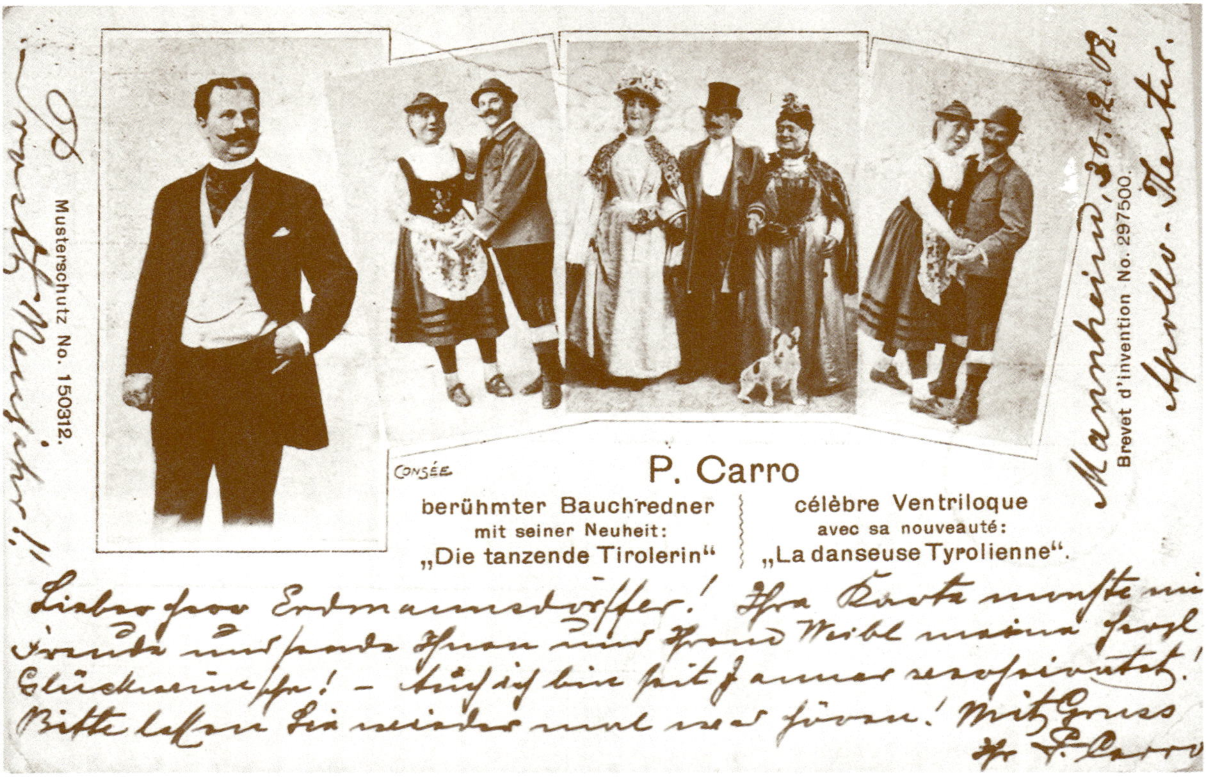
Musterschutz No. 150312.
CONSÉE
P. Carro
berühmter Bauchredner
mit seiner Neuheit:
„Die tanzende Tirolerin"
célèbre Ventriloque
avec sa nouveauté:
„La danseuse Tyrolienne".
Brevet d'invention No. 297500.

Fred Cecil

FRED VALLANCE.

NELSON HARDY,
8, Chivalry Road, Wandsworth Common, S.W.
524 Battersea

.. ADELER & SUTTON'S PIERROTS ...

TELEPHONE
No. 2058.
ALSO OF THE
QUEEN'S HALL CONCERTS, LONDON.

JOHN GODDARD,
30 COLLEGE AVENUE,
LEICESTER.

Yours truly, Grieve, Ventriloquist.

CHARLES CONYERS AND HIS FRIEND TOMMY TROTTERS.

PROFESSOR VALENTINE,
THE YORKSHIRE VENTRILOQUIST.
IN "THE PHRENOLOGIST" AND "ONLY A DREAM."
TERMS: 28, THEAKER LANE, ARMLEY.

9

I CAN SEE YOUR LIPS MOVING

Facing: Paul Winchell and Jerry Mahoney. In the fifties, Paul Winchell became to viewing audiences what Edgar Bergen had been to the listening ones. The program "Winchell/Mahoney Time" was one of the most innovative shows of the decade. Winchell's multi-talent not only brought new ways to infuse life into his wooden characters, but also his fellow man. In the early sixties, he invented and patented the design for the artificial human heart.[1a]

Below: Bill, the ventriloquial head which, on October 2nd, 1925, was the first object ever televised by John Logie Baird. Later, in 1928, Bill became the first image to be transmitted across the Atlantic.

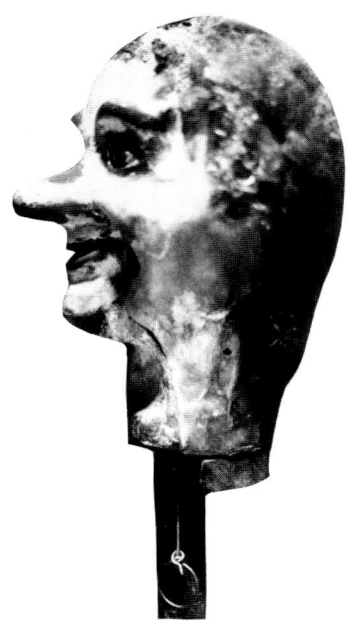

By the early 1950s, television had edged its way to the footlights, presenting the final challenge to ventriloquism. The question was whether or not this art could withstand the savage scrutiny of the T.V. camera which treated so many of the performing arts without mercy. In television, a more subtle approach and the refining of certain techniques were required, particularly lip control, which has become the prime factor in the audience's assessment of the art.

The animated part of the ventriloquial act made a television appearance long before the human side. In 1925, when John Logie Baird began his experimental transmissions, he used a ventriloquial head given to him by Arthur Prince. This was in answer to journalists who told Baird that, in order to make his invention newsworthy, they would have to see a subject on the screen—a being. With this in mind Baird obtained the head, which he named Bill. On February 8, 1928, Bill's head became the first image to be transmitted across the Atlantic when it was picked up by a receiving station in Hartsdale, New York.[1]

Arthur Prince was the first ventriloquist to present the art on television, during experimental transmission of the Baird system. Then, on November 7, 1936, he headed the first television variety show broadcast from *Alexandra Palace* during the inauguration

Arthur Prince and Jim performing in front of the Baird television apparatus during an experimental broadcast in 1925.

Below: Albert Saveen with his female character Daisy May and his talking dog Micky.

Below Right: Terry Hall with Lenny the Lion.

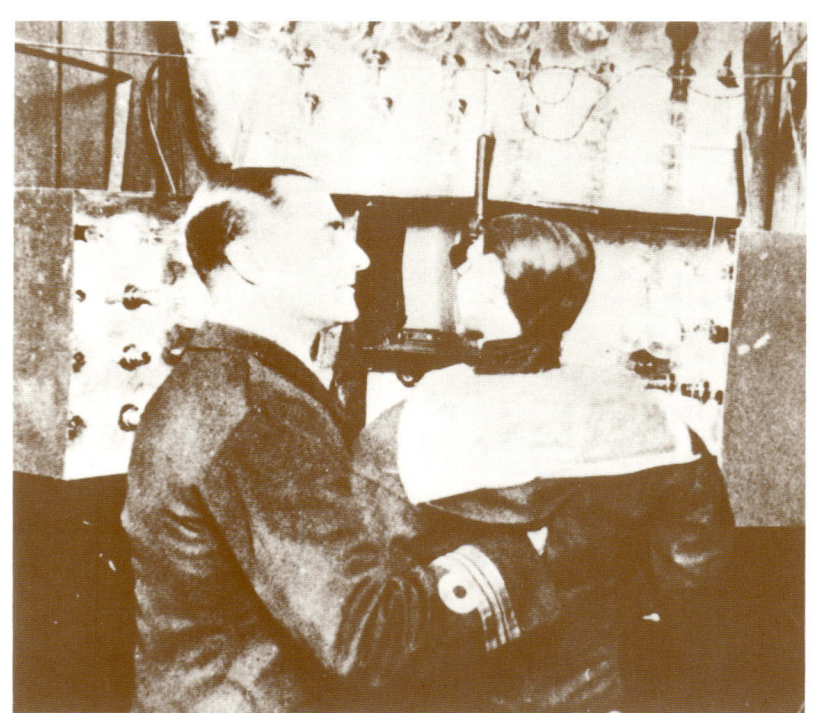

week of Britain's first television station. The show, *Cabaret*, came into being long before the invention of videotape recordings; it went on the air 'live' at 3:30 pm, and was repeated the same evening at 10:30 pm.[2]

A.C. Astor, Johnson Clarke and Senor Wences also appeared on the small screen during these early days of television broadcasting in Britain, and continued to do so until 1939, when transmissions were suspended because of the outbreak of war. After television broadcasts resumed in the mid 1940s, many ventriloquists began appearing on this new medium, and programs such as *Cabaret* and *Music Hall* became a window display for variety entertainment.

In the early fifties, younger viewers in Britain tuned into B.B.C.'s *Children's Hour* which featured two programs starring ventriloquists Albert Saveen and Francis Coudrill.

Albert Saveen charmed audiences with his coy female character Daisy May and the comic antics of the precocious spiv, Andy.[3] By contrast, on Saturday mornings, Francis Coudrill brought a sense of adventure with Hank, a cowboy who told of his wild west adventures with the aid of clever visual animation drawn by Coudrill.[4]

With the introduction of commercial television in Britain (1954), ventriloquist Terry Hall retired his boy figure Micky

Below left: Ray Alan who has the distinction of being the first ventriloquist to age his aristocratic figure, Lord Charles.

Below right: Keith Harris with his bird figure Orville. It is rare for ventriloquists to penetrate the commercial side of show business, but in 1982 Keith Harris made an unprecedented breakthrough into the British music charts and shot into the Top Ten with Orville's song, which sold over 350,000 copies.

Dennis Spicer with James Green.

Below: *Jeff Dunham and his grumpy old man, Walter.*

Flynn and replaced him with a lion puppet called Lenny. After successful guest appearances on sponsored television, the duo gained enormous exposure through a series of commercials for a candy mint. They later starred in their own program for B.B.C.[5]

In North America, the most coveted showcase for variety performers was Ed Sullivan's *Toast of the Town*, which eventually became the *Ed Sullivan Show*.[6] During its record run of twenty-two years it presented speciality acts from around the world. These included ventriloquists of almost every nationality. Spanish ventriloquist Senor Wences, who became internationally famous, made guest appearances on the show throughout most of its run. Wences, who combines the art of juggling with ventriloquism, is renowned for his head-in-the-box character Pedro, and for his talking hand character Johnny. His amusing catch-phrases, 'Deefeecult for you, easy for me', and 'S-o.k. S-all-right', became so popular that they eventually resulted in the production of a record using the latter phrase as the title. Adept at distant voice ventriloquism, Wences once startled a priest in Spain during the christening of a friend's baby. As the priest sprinkled water on to the infant's head, a tiny voice was heard to say, 'Oh, father, the water is cold.'[7]

Among prominent British artists to feature on the Ed Sullivan show were Arthur Worsley and Denis Spicer. Worsley began his career at eleven, and by the time he was fourteen, he was playing at most of Britain's principal theatres, billed as 'the world's youngest ventriloquist'. His unique presentation as the 'mute ventriloquist' brought him international recognition. Throughout his act, Worsley remains silent, allowing his figure Charlie Brown to do all the talking, evoking laughter and applause through his articulate pronunciation of consonant sounds.

Denis Spicer was also a superb technician and possessed a remarkable repertoire, rarely appearing with the same act twice. His regular characters, James Green and Maxwell the Monkey, were great favorites with the viewing public. In 1966, Spicer was chosen for the Royal Variety Performance and for the occasion he made a small dog figure, a parody of the Queen's corgis. Tragically, less than two weeks after the show, Spicer was the victim of a fatal car accident. Police at the scene found a small shoe and, not knowing the driver's identity, they feared a child had been trapped in the wreckage. It was later discovered that the shoe belonged to Spicer's figure James Green.[8]

Apart from the stand-up routines, many ventriloquists began to use television more fully, presenting their art in specially written situation sketches. American ventriloquist Paul Winchell

Above: Ed Sullivan and his 'really big shew' with Ricky Layne and Vevel in 1966. Ventriloquist Ricky Layne appeared on the show 48 times with his figure Vevel, who engaged in regular comic exchanges with Sullivan.[9]

Left: Jay Marshall with his 'talking hand' character Leftie.
Right: Arthur Worsley, 'the mute ventriloquist', with Charlie Brown. Marshall and Worsley were frequent performers on the Ed Sullivan Show.

Right: Shari Lewis, international television star, with her famous character Lamb Chop.

Below: Ventro-impressionist, Clifford Guest, with his baby figure. Guest is famous for his distant voice technique which he features as the main part of his act.

was one of the first artists to feature in this type of format. Winchell, a former polio victim, taught himself ventriloquism while confined to a hospital bed. Shortly after he recovered, he entered and won the first prize on radio's *Major Bowes Amateur Hour* and from there he turned professional. After his television debut in 1947 on the *Ed Sullivan Show*, Winchell began to feature on a regular program with his character Jerry Mahoney, eventually becoming to viewers what Edgar Bergen had been to listeners.[10]

In the fifties this nationally broadcast series called *The Paul Winchell-Jerry Mahoney Show* (1950-54) became one of the most innovative programs of the decade with host Paul Winchell acting, singing and dancing his way through weekly situations that also involved guest celebrities. During this period, Winchell introduced another wooden side-kick, Knucklehead Smiff, although his star character Jerry Mahoney remained the viewer's favorite.[11]

During the early seventies, the demand for nostalgia prompted Winchell to organize the re-release of the shows for a new generation of young viewers through the home video market. But the television station KTTV, where the show was made, would not release the master tapes, although Winchell owned them and the broadcast rights.

In the dog-in-the-manger dispute which followed, KTTV took it upon itself to erase all the master tapes of the Winchell-Mahoney shows and thereby bring the matter to a close.

It took seventeen years of legal battle before Paul Winchell could gain restitution for this malicious act. In 1989 the case was taken to Court and during the hearing the white-haired Winchell took out his retired Jerry Mahoney from his suitcase and presented him to the jury. Jerry told Winchell that he felt comfortable in the court room because he had seen a relative. When Winchell inquired who it was, Jerry told him that it was the Judge's wooden gavel. 'We come from the same family, you know.'

The lawyer for Metro Media who owned KTTV was infuriated by these dramatics, which he called 'crude, slapstick humor.' But the poignancy of what had happened was brought to life by the appearance of the Winchell-Mahoney team which many of the jury had grown up with in their living rooms. The Winchell-Mahoney Show had become as much a part of Americana as Bergen/McCarthy, *Howdy Doody* and *Kaptain Kangaroo*. It was an American legacy that had been snatched from them forever. The jury found KTTV guilty of what was later described as 'the most malicious act of cultural vandalism in recent American history'. Paul Winchell was awarded 14.8 million in damages.[12]

Both Bergen and Brough made the transition from radio to television. Edgar Bergen played host on *Do You Trust Your Wife?*[13] and, much later, Peter Brough presented a televised version of his radio success, *Educating Archie*. Jimmy Nelson became nationally famous after his debut on the *Milton Berle Texaco Show*, where he featured his characters Danny O'Day, Humphrey Higsby and Farfel the Dog. Nelson is renowned for his rapid voice change technique and has remained in the viewing public's eye through his widely syndicated commercial for Nestles.[14]

Although many ventriloquists incorporate distant voice ventriloquism into their acts, unlike their predecessors, few feature this as a main part of their entertainment. Australian-born Clifford Guest is one of the exceptions, demonstrating the sounds of a fox hunt where the horses, riders and hounds are heard gradually fading into the distance. Guest, who is billed as a 'ventro-impressionist', also features many modern sounds, such as the simulation of a jet plane and rocket lift-off.[15]

Many ventriloquists have redesigned their presentations especially for television. The multi-talented Shari Lewis, who first employed two conventional figures, eventually brought to the

In 1949, Shirley Dinsdale hosted her own children's program on the NBC network with her saucy pigtailed figure 'Judy Splinters.' The 21-year-old ventriloquiste became the first person ever to win the coveted Emmy award.[16]

Below: Willie Tyler and Lester, who are great favorites with American viewers, presenting their hip humor and exceptional singing numbers.[17]

Above: Swiss ventriloquist Daniel Remy.
Facing: The great Robert Lamouret, who would sing Italian arias while the comic antics of his duck 'Duddles' would steal the show.
Below left: Fred Robey with his dog Miki.
Below right: George Schlick, famous for his talking armor mask which interjects throughout Schlick's act.

screen her much admired family of hand puppets Lamb Chop, Charlie Horse and Hush Puppy. Her versatility as a singer, dancer and ventriloquiste have made her a television star on both sides of the Atlantic.[18]

Although television has become the showcase for the variety artist, live entertainment is still in demand and ventriloquism remains a popular, though infrequent, entertainment, particularly in club and cabaret circles. In 1947 French cabaret artist Robert Lamouret was introduced to the English-speaking audience via the *Sid Fields Show* at the Haymarket Theatre,[19] London, and later seen on the *Ed Sullivan Show*. Lamouret's act, which was reviewed as 'sensational', relied more upon visual movement than dialogue, bringing forward a new aspect of the ventriloquial art. Employing a small duck figure Duddles, fashioned after the famous Disney cartoon character Donald Duck, Lamouret concentrated more upon its manipulation than its vocal aspects. This not only proved an asset in performing to an international audience, but through Lamouret's acute sense of timing and clever inventiveness, the figure appeared to change expression with its actions. One of the highlights of this now classic routine was when the duck lost one of its eyes, which Lamouret would find and inadvertently place on the wrong side of its face.

Jane and Mary Donskaji, Russian ventriloquistes, with Andrea, their boy figure. Following the tradition of her grandfather, Georgori Donskaji, who performed in Russia for more than sixty years, Mary is the third generation to practise the art.

Right: The Rev. Ichiro Noda, Japan's most prominent ventriloquist. Although the art is relatively new in the Orient, the Rev. Ichiro Noda runs a school in which he teaches ventriloquism. As in many of the arts in Japan, when a student graduates he adopts his teacher's name as a mark of his achievement.

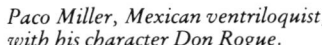

Paco Miller, Mexican ventriloquist, with his character Don Rogue.

Because of its international appeal, this whittling down of dialogue in favor of rhythmic vocal changes, such as Wences' 'Ss-ok, ss-all-right' and amusing actions with the more pliable hand or glove puppets, has found particular favor with international cabaret artists. Among the many European ventriloquists who have adopted this type of presentation are George Schlick with his talking armour head and Daniel Remy, whose visual business includes assembling his bird figure before the audience. Another European artist to gain international prominence is Fred Roby, one of the few ventriloquists in recent years to have publicly performed in Russia. Although Roby did not speak Russian, his clever visual activity of drinking, smoking and playing a harmonica while his figure sang received a standing ovation in Moscow.

While many think of ventriloquism as being peculiar to the Western world, it is a performing art that is practiced in almost every country. In Russia, it is seen as part of the traditional circus, and in Japan as a modern extension of the ancient puppet theatre. Ventriloquial performers in Spain have always enjoyed popularity and Senor Balder was perhaps the country's most outstanding exponent. Eugenio Balder employed a repertoire of twentyeight figures which were not caricatures but lifelike reproductions. Balder's skilful manipulation of these automatons led the audience to believe that they were flesh and blood. A favorite was

Cleto, a life-sized figure which engaged Balder in a bout of Grecian wrestling that eventually found the ventriloquist flat on his back.

Another skilful presentation was his La Orquestra Criolla, engaging six figures which played various instruments. The masks for Balder's figures were sculptured by Juanito Paceco, although Balder added the intricate movements. Balder wrote several books on ventriloquism and performed for some fifty years until his death in 1964.[21]

When ventriloquism was married to puppetry and the ventriloquist embodied the 'familiar' in a visible partner, this not only popularized the art but also made heroes of many animated figures such as Fred Russell's Joe, Arthur Prince's Jim, and Edgar Bergen's Charlie McCarthy, which *Time* magazine called 'the most famous animated character in history'.[22] Today, this mantle has been passed on to Jim Henson's Muppets who, through the medium of television, are seen by over 250 million people around the world. Muppets (Henson's own word, combining 'marionette' and 'puppet') are essentially made for the screen, often requiring up to five people to operate one character. Fully using the medium of television, Henson and his team of puppeteers have taken the animation to its zenith, enabling the characters to move without any apparent restriction.[23]

The Muppet Show appeals to every age group and involves human guests along with the animated figures who exchange dialogue in a ventriloquial-type situation. Many of these characters, such as Kermit the Frog and Miss Piggy, have become just as popular as Mickey Mouse and Donald Duck. Like Disney, the Henson organization favors animal characters, and the Muppets have greatly influenced the style of the animated figure. Many ventriloquists now favor the more flexible type of figure made from materials such as foam rubber and acrylics.

Jim Henson, the creator of the Muppets, was first inspired when, as a teenager, he listened to the Bergen and McCarthy broadcasts in the 1940s. His desire to emulate Bergen prompted him to create his own puppet characters, and he eventually got his break on a local television station in Washington D.C. where he appeared on a late night slot. Unlike ventriloquists who share the limelight with their partners, Henson preferred to remain invisible as a puppeteer. After many years he eventually made his family of Muppets a household word through the award-winning program, *Sesame Street*. Always a great admirer of Bergen's work, in 1978 Henson invited his mentor to appear on the *Muppet Show* and later featured the famous Bergen-McCarthy duo in *The Muppet*

Jim Henson with Kermit, his muppet character.

Below: *Ronn Lucas and his firebreathing dragon Scorch. Lucas and his larger-than-life characters have become favorites with viewing audiences on both sides of the Atlantic.*[18]

Movie. Shortly before the film was due for release, Bergen died and Henson, as a final tribute, decided to dedicate the movie 'to the magic and memory of Edgar Bergen'.

At Edgar Bergen's memorial service in Hollywood, Henson and Kermit were invited to say a few words at the request of the ventriloquist's widow Frances and daughter Candice. After a few exchanges with Kermit, Henson said, 'Edgar Bergen's work with Charlie and Mortimer was magic in the real sense. Something happened when Edgar spoke through Charlie. Things were said that couldn't be said by ordinary people. We of the Muppets, as well as many others, are continuing in his footsteps. We're part of the cycle. We take up where he left off and we thank him for leaving this delightful legacy of love and humor and whimsy'.[24]

Puppeteers, like ventriloquists, invite the audience to indulge in a world of fantasy and make-believe. Embellishing their performances with wit, humor and sentiment, both persuade the audience to accept the existence of their character creations.

Ventriloquists distinguish themselves from puppeteers by *visibly* exchanging dialogue with their animated figures. This is essentially the art of ventriloquism—the ability to create other voices and, more importantly, other personalities divorced from one's own. Then, by skilful misdirection, the ventriloquist transposes these characteristics to the animated figure, completing the illusion of its independent existence. Incorporating these techniques of misdirection and animation, ventriloquism combines the art of the magician and the puppeteer.

Spanish ventriloquist Jose Luis Moreno with his crow figure, Rockefeller. Moreno comes from a family of ventriloquists. His uncle is Senor Wences, whose brother Senor Moreno also practiced the art.

Facing: A promotional record poster showing Senor Balder with his colorful family of figures.

Below: Marie Carmen, who in recent years has become the most popular ventriloquial artist in Spain. Employing five figures, her homogeneous humor cleverly satirizes Spanish life.

In his parody, veteran comedian Sandy Powell as 'the world's worst ventriloquist'.

Below: 'Soap', the television parody of the American soap opera, with ventriloquist Jay Johnson and Bob, his mouthpiece, battling with Bert Cambell. (Richard Mulligan)

Today, ventriloquism is viewed by many as an oddity left over from the vaudeville days, and the familiar image of the artist carrying a mouth-moving figure seems to typify that era, being constantly parodied by the satirist. One of the most renowned parodies on the art in recent years was British comic Sandy Powell's presentation of 'the world's worst ventriloquist'. Powell, a veteran comedian, appeared on stage dressed in a military uniform as a caricature of Coram, and worked a standard figure through which he would attempt to ventriloquize.

The satirical cartoonist has also cleverly employed the art over the years, often drawing political figures manipulating or being manipulated. The earliest cartoon to feature this approach was printed in the German newspaper, *Der Kladdadast*, during Cole's appearances in 1881. The cartoon showed Cole operating the German Parliament with the caption, 'Even Prince Bismarck would enjoy Cole, his wonderful voice and command over his assembly who only say what he puts into their mouths'.[25]

As well as being used for entertainment, in recent years ventriloquism has been channelled into other avenues. For example, psychiatrists and social workers have used the practice as a teaching method for the mentally handicapped child who often finds empathy with the animated figure. The art has also retraced its steps back into the religious arena being currently engaged by a growing number of *gospel vents*.

Ventriloquism is said to be a dying art but, emerging from religious mysticism to a specialized form of entertainment, it has triumphantly survived the test of time. The ancient ventriloquists created an aura of wonderment as they sought the future by evoking the spirits of the past. Today, although the modern ventriloquists cannot, of course, predict the future, they can perhaps, through their special skill, continue to bring hope by evoking the unifying spirit of laughter.

The Rev. Philip Scofield who, in 1948, astonished his fellow Anglicans and made headlines when he took Johnny, his 'familiar', into the pulpit. Today, gospel-vents are a frequent feature in many religious organizations around the world.

B.C.   BY JOHNNY HART

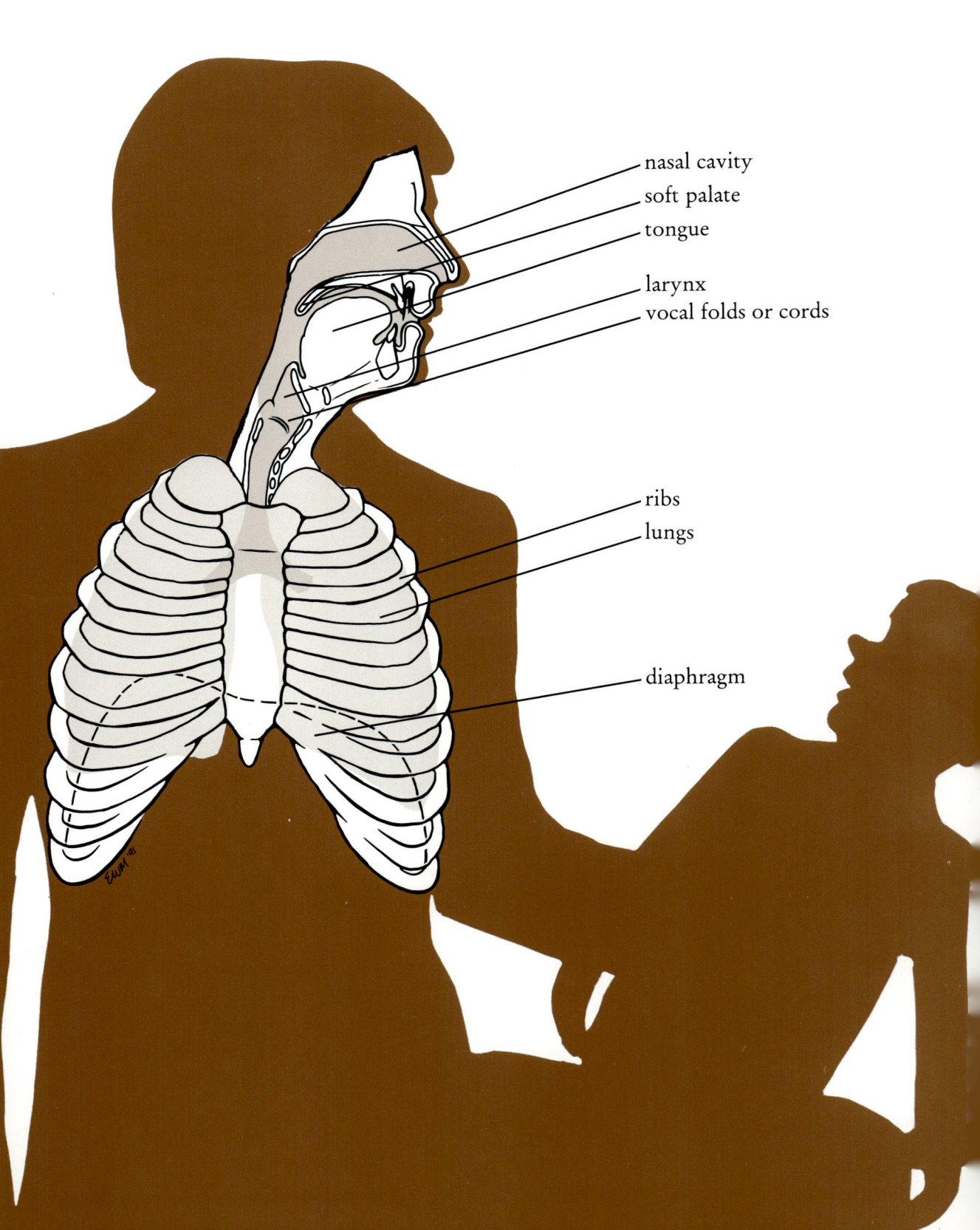

10

LET ME OUT

Facing: A diagram of the vocal and respiratory mechanism.
Diagram by Elizabeth Weadon Massari.

While ventriloquists have been comparatively few in number, the art of ventriloquism can be acquired and it is not, as commonly believed, a gift bestowed upon certain individuals. This view was largely propagated by Victorian ventriloquists who wanted to be observed as superhuman, possessing vocal powers beyond the reach of any normal being. Walter Cole claimed, 'If a man is not born a ventriloquist, he will never become one'. He also stated that a physical abnormality was required, saying, 'It is a peculiar formation of the throat muscles'.[1]

Like Cole, many ventriloquists at that time preferred to be regarded as having an unusual talent that enabled them to 'throw the voice'. The fallacy that the voice can be thrown was largely publicized by ventriloquists themselves and later supported by the numerous heroes in boys' books and comics who were sometimes given the superhuman ability of tossing their voices anywhere within hearing.[2]

The word 'ventriloquist', meaning belly speaker, has also contributed to much of the confusion surrounding the practice. Ventriloquial sounds are not made in the stomach as implied by the name, but by the vocal organs normally engaged in producing sounds. This misnomer prompted Mr. Love to call himself a polyphonist (imitator of sounds), feeling it was a better explan-

Below: A ten cent 'how to do it' book on ventriloquism by Harry Kennedy. (1898)

BOYS! BOYS! BOYS!
THROW YOUR VOICE

Into a trunk, under the bed, under a table back of the door, into a desk at school, or anywhere. You get lots of fun fooling the teacher, policeman, peddlers, and surprise and fool all your friends besides.

THE VENTRILO

is a little instrument that fits in the mouth out of sight. Cannot be detected. It is used in connection with the above, and with the aid of this wonderful **DOUBLE THROAT or VENTRILO,** you can imitate all kinds of birds, animals, etc. Remember you get everything for **ONLY TEN CENTS**—a 32 page book giving you full instructions how to become a ventriloquist and throw your voice, and the Double Throat, or Ventrilo, besides.

No. 3461. Ventrilo & 32 Page Book............10c

Above: The advertisement that became every boy's dream, which promised voice throwing ability for only ten cents.

Right: The Great Lester teaching the art in his Hollywood studio in the fifties.

ation of the art.³ Mimicry is the root of the practice, according to W.F. Pinchbeck, in his work published in 1800. He wrote, 'So you want to be a ventriloquist? Learn to be a mimic and you will easily effect your purpose'.⁴

The art is based upon the fact that the ear experiences great difficulty in determining the exact source of the sounds that it hears. 'It seems too near to be so faint', or, 'It seemed too loud to come from so far', are familiar apologies for errors in judging the distance and the source of sounds. The ventriloquist takes advantage of this human handicap by mimicking near and distant sounds while misdirecting the auditor. It is a vocal illusion; the ventriloquist deceives the ear as the magician deceives the eye. But, unlike magic, ventriloquism requires no secretive presentation. If a magician were to reveal to the audience how a trick or illusion is done, the performance would cease to be credible. Ventriloquism, on the other hand, relies solely upon the ability to imitate near or distant sound, and where a figure is employed, to infuse it with life and character.

Contrary to popular belief, ventriloquism requires no special endowment, no physical abnormality or superhuman ability; it can be acquired by application. It is generally a self-taught art, although there have been teachers and schools devoted to its practice. At the beginning of the nineteenth century, Christopher Sugg taught the art, and among his students was the actor and mimic, Charles Matthews. During the 1950s, the Great Lester ran a studio in Hollywood where he held daily classes.⁵

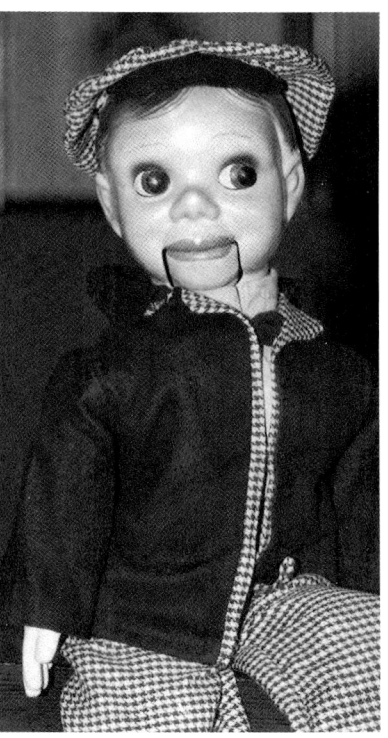

Below: Willie Talk, that was produced for Sears Robuck Company in 1925 for budding ventriloquists.

Since ventriloquism has become an entertainment, hundreds of 'how to do it' books have been written on the subject. Many of these works often promise voice throwing ability within hours, some by the use of a metal aid inserted into the mouth. However, the properly informative books have correctly advised that ventriloquism is attained by application and practice.

In one of the earliest instructional books, *'A Treatise on Ventriloquism'* published in 1833, George Sutton said, 'To bring a feat of ventriloquism to the perfection of all beholders, a constant and unlimited practice is needed'.⁶ Practice is the root to accomplishing the art, and while there are no special requisites, there are certain fundamental guidelines. The key factors in producing the ventriloquial illusion are the ventriloquial voice, lip control and misdirection.

The art falls into two main categories, near ventriloquism and distant voice ventriloquism. *Near ventriloquism* is the term applied when a ventriloquist performs with a figure. It is so called because of the proximity of the figure from which the ventriloquial sound appears to proceed. *Distant voice ventriloquism* is the term used when the ventriloquial voice appears to come from a distance—outside, upstairs, below the floor or off-stage.

To understand how the ventriloquial sound is made, it is necessary to examine the mechanics of normal voice production. In producing the normal voice three mechanical elements are involved—a motivating force, the breath, a vibrator, the vocal folds, and finally a resonator, the throat, nose and mouth cavity.

The breath from the lungs is passed through the larynx or 'voice box', which is situated in the neck. In the larynx are two ligaments known as vocal folds or cords. When the air from the lungs passes over these, it causes them to vibrate, producing tone. In turn, this tone moves to the resonators, where it is resounded and amplified. From there it is the function of the articulators, the tongue, teeth and lips, to mold the tone into recognizable speech.

While all functions of the vocal mechanism are as important as each other, the only actively working agent is the breathing

Below: The Great Lester and Edgar Bergen with Charlie McCarthy. When Lester opened his studio in Hollywood, Edgar Bergen, feeling that his technique had become rusty, enrolled in Lester's school. Lester holds Broadway Eddy, the later figure he used after retiring Frank Byron, Jr.

mechanism. Because of this, the production of a satisfactory voice is greatly dependent upon good breathing habits. Breathing is the power behind the voice and, if the voice is to reach its highest efficiency, it is necessary to learn to handle this motive power with as little struggle as possible.

It may seem that we need no training for breathing, as we breathe constantly in order to live. However, breathing for life is periodic, the inhalation and exhalation taking almost the same amount of time. Breathing for the voice requires management, often necessitating a quick intake of breath and then a retention of sufficient breath to support the tone throughout the speaking period.

The lungs are the essential organs of respiration. The air is drawn into the lungs as the size of the chest is increased and, when expelled, it provides a stream of air that passes over the vocal mechanism necessary for speech.

Apart from the lungs, nature has provided an additional aid for respiration, namely the muscular breathing system consisting of the inspiratory and expiratory muscles, i.e. the thorax and the diaphragm. The latter is a large fibro-muscular partition between the lung and abdominal cavities. It is dome-shaped to conform with the concave base of the lungs. During inhalation, the diaphragm is active and contracts as the abdominal muscles yield, by relaxing. When breathing out, the diaphragm is passive and returns to its arched position, assisting the lungs in exhalation.

Although the activity of the lungs and diaphragm is automatic,

---

The Original Great Lester
(Not the magician)

World's Famous Ventriloquist of International Fame

— NOW TEACHING —

The True Art of Ventriloquism
IN ALL ITS BRANCHES

**Distant Voices, Stunts, Tricks, and Business
Also Professional Coaching**

Personal Instructions Only — Moderate Prices

Self-addressed stamped envelope for reply

GREAT LESTER
Studios 1 & 2 — 5540 Hollywood Boulevard
HOLLYWOOD 28, CALIFORNIA

Satisfactory results guaranteed or money refunded

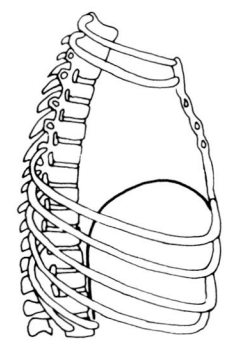

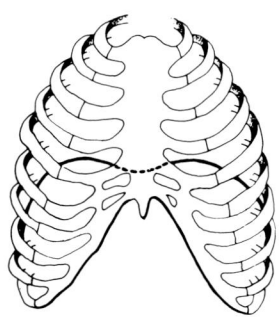

The above illustrations show the active and passive positions of the diaphragm.

these organs can be controlled, and it is by voluntarily doing so that one can add power to the breath, gaining firm and sensitive control over the voice.

The first step in attaining control over the respiratory system is to become physically familiar with its functions. A simple experiment is to lie flat on the back and place the fingers lightly above the waist on the soft part between the ribs. Breathe naturally and note the movement of the diaphragm. Try the same experiment sitting upright on a chair. When inhaling the stomach muscles should yield and move outwards and when exhaling the fingers should feel the ascent of the diaphragm. Care should be taken throughout these exercises not to raise the shoulders or the ribs during inhalation.

A further experiment is to separate the two movements. A full intake of breath is admitted, using the simultaneous movements of the ribs and diaphragm. The breath is then emitted by raising the diaphragm alone, after which the ribs are allowed to descend. Another exercise is to expand the ribcage and then inhale and exhale, using the diaphragm only. This exercise is sometimes found difficult at first, but it will be achieved with perseverance. This method of control is called rib-reserve, as the maintained elevation of the ribs holds back a reserve air supply which can be used at will.

The controlling of the motivating force is invaluable to any vocal performer, particularly the ventriloquist, whose art requires the diversified use of the vocal mechanism.

The Ventriloquial Voice

When ventriloquists perform with a figure they produce two voices—their own natural speaking voice and the voice for the figure, known as the near-ventriloquial voice. The two differ, and this vocal contrast is the first step in creating the ventriloquial illusion.

The near-ventriloquial voice is produced by a peculiar positioning of the tongue. In normal speech, the tongue lies flat and the tone passes over it, mainly through the mouth and partly through the nose cavity. When speaking in the ventriloquial voice, the performer reverses this action by arching the back of the tongue. In this position, the tone is deflected so that it passes mainly through the nose cavity and partially through the mouth. This positioning of the tongue can be found by making the 'ng' sound as in words such as sang, song, wring, fling, etc. The back of the tongue makes contact with the soft palate, giving the voice a certain vibrant nasal quality.

Making a prolonged 'Ah' sound while changing the tongue from the flat to the arched position, will clarify the difference in sounds. This is often referred to as the ventriloquial drone.

In his work, *How to Become a Ventriloquist,* Edgar Bergen wrote, 'When you have mastered the drone, the next step is to learn to change rapidly and smoothly from your own voice to the drone'.[7] Practice this change first with letters, then with words, and finally with sentences. The nature of the ventriloquial voice will depend on the character the performer is trying to create. Possibly the most popular voice has been the 'cheeky boy' character, such as Charlie McCarthy and Archie Andrews. The voice of the latter was described by Peter Brough as 'the thin treble of a fourteen-year-old boy'.[8]

Whatever the chosen voice, its effectiveness will depend upon the individual ability of the ventriloquist to modify the voice to suit the character, remembering that the greater the contrast in the two voices, the more complete the illusion. The choice of the right voice to fit the character is often made through trial and error. When Terry Hall first created Lenny the Lion, he gave the animal figure a deep roaring voice, which he felt was suitable for the creation. But on stage, this voice did not bring the response that he had hoped for. Later, at the suggestion of singer Ann Shelton, he gave the lion a rather effeminate voice. This comical contrast proved to be the ingredient which helped make Lenny the Lion into a national character.

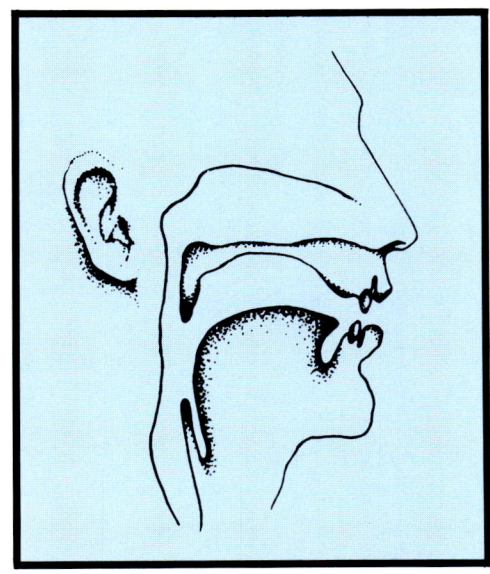

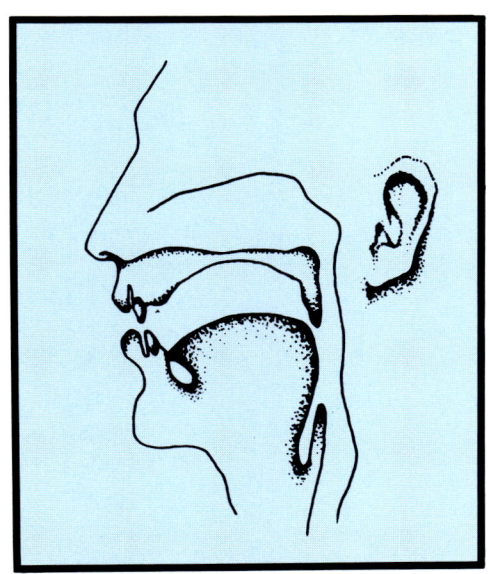

Below left: The position of the tongue in normal speech.

Below right: The position of the tongue in ventriloquial speech.

A portrait of E.D. Davies in 1880. Ventriloquists often grew a large moustache to hide any lip movement.

Lip Control

Lip control is possibly the greatest contributor in creating the ventriloquial illusion. When Joseph Askins appeared at the Sadler's Wells Theatre in 1796, a line in the advertisement announcing his performance read, 'nor will the closest observer be able to discover any motion of the lips or alteration of features, the only true test of being a genuine ventriloquist'.[9]

To most people, ventriloquism *is* the art of speaking without moving the lips, and although many other important techniques are necessary to master the practice, lip control has become the universal criterion of a good or a bad ventriloquist. When a ventriloquist performs, the observer is challenged to see if the lips move, and competence at the technique has become the most important factor in an audience assessment of his art. The scrutiny of the television camera has presented an even greater challenge to this technique.

Many early exponents felt that not all speech sounds could be pronounced without moving the lips. Frederick Maccabe wrote, 'It would be sometimes necessary for the ventriloquist to turn his head away from the audience while attempting certain consonants'.[10] George Sutton also held this view, saying, 'The conversation should be arranged so that the letters B, P, F, M, V are seldom, if ever, used'.[11] Many ventriloquists in the nineteenth century often grew large moustaches or smoked continuously in an attempt to cover up their incompetence. The press was quick to praise a ventriloquist who appeared 'clean shaven', as they did with Fred Russell, Walter Cole and Arthur Prince. In his work *The Whole Art of Ventriloquism*, Prince stated that it *is* possible to pronounce all speech sounds with comparative clarity.[12] This has since been proved many times by ventriloquists who have included the difficult consonant sounds as a focal point of their performances.

Speech is the articulate joining together of vowels and consonants. The organs of articulation are the tongue, teeth, velum and lips. It is the function of all these articulators to mold the tone into recognizable speech. In normal speech, to have clear and acceptable diction, all these articulators must be ready to respond. For the ventriloquial voice, the ventriloquist must engage only the interior articulators while keeping the visible, exterior ones immobile. This constitutes no difficulty in pronouncing the vowel sounds A, E, I, O, U. With the teeth and lips slightly apart, to allow passage for sound, the vowels are easily pronounced using only the tongue and interior organs of the mouth, without any motion of the lips or facial muscles.

However, this is not the case with the consonants B, P, F, M and V, because these are speech sounds in which the breath is impeded, diverted or stopped in expiration by particular use of the lips.

For instance, to pronounce the sound F, the upper teeth and lower lip meet and form a partial obstruction so that the sound is impeded. For the nasal sound M, the lips are closed and the sound is diverted through the nose, and for P, the lips are tightly closed until there is a build-up of pressure. The breath is then stopped and momentarily released, completing the consonant.

To overcome the problem of enunciating the consonants without moving the lips, the ventriloquist must learn to duplicate their sounds using only the interior organs of the mouth which are unseen by the observer. For full understanding of this method it is necessary to examine how these consonants are normally produced.

In the 40's the popularity of Charlie McCarthy prompted toy manufacturers to offer a variety of ventriloquist figures for beginners.

B and P

B and P are stop plosives. They are formed by a complete closure of the lips, followed by a sudden parting which allows the concentrated air to escape. The difference in pronouncing the two is that B is voiced while P is voiceless. A voiced sound is one in which there is a vocal fold vibration during production. With the voiceless sound there is no vibration of the vocal folds. This difference can easily be noted by placing the fingers lightly against the larynx (Adam's apple) and making the voiceless sound P and the voiced sound B.

To pronounce B and P ventriloquially, it is necessary to duplicate the explosive quality of both consonants. For this, the tip of the tongue is brought into contact with the upper front teeth at the point at which they meet the gum ridge. As with normal pronunciation, there is a blockage of air then a sudden parting of the tongue from its position, releasing the impounded breath.

For the correct pronunciation, the B is voiced, while the P is made by the emission of air only. With the P consonant care should be taken not to use an undue amount of breath, but enough to make the sound accurate.

In making these sounds ventriloquially, using the above method, there is a tendency among many performers to pronounce them as T and D so that 'bad boy' sounds like 'dad doy' and 'polly parrot' is like 'tolly tarrot'. The different positioning of the tongue for pronouncing T and D normally and the ventriloquial P and B should be carefully noted.

In normal speech, to make the voiced D and the voiceless T, the rim of the tongue forms a blockage of air when it is pressed firmly against the gum ridge. When it is released from this position the sound is completed.

The positioning of the tongue for pronouncing B and P ventriloquially is slightly more forward on to the gum ridge so that the tip of the tongue is touching the upper front teeth. The distinction may be noted by slowly pronouncing words like 'Peter' which require both tongue positions.

F and V

In the production of the fricative consonants F and V, the breath stream is continuous, but as the air escapes through the narrow opening some audible friction takes place. Both are formed by a light contact between the elevated lower lip and the cutting edges of the upper front teeth.

Ventriloquially, these consonants present little difficulty, and

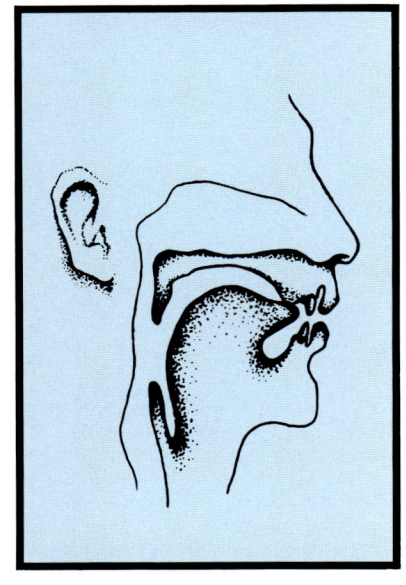

The position of the tongue for pronouncing the letter D normally. This is often confused with the ventriloquial position for pronouncing B and P.

many performers find that with practice they can pronounce these sounds accurately without any particular positioning of the tongue. Alternatively, for the F sound, the tip of the tongue touches lightly against the upper front teeth and the breath is allowed to pass through this narrow opening. The same operation applies to V, except that the sound is voiced.

Another method of producing these fricatives ventriloquially without lip movement is to rest the upper front teeth lightly on the lower lip and, through this contact point, make the characteristic sounds. For each method, the breath must be controlled so as not to agitate the lips, causing visible movement.

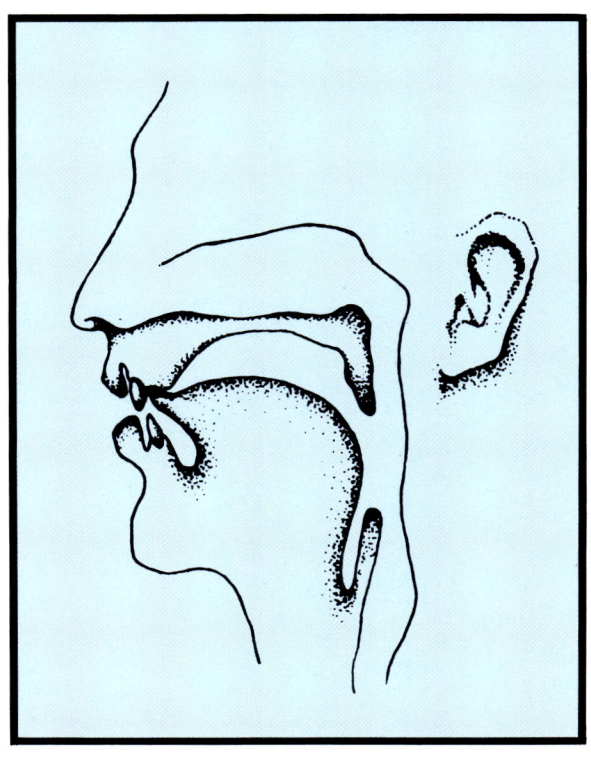

The position of the tongue for pronouncing the consonants P and B. To make their characteristic sound the tongue is parted from this position, releasing the impounded breath. B is voiced while P is voiceless.

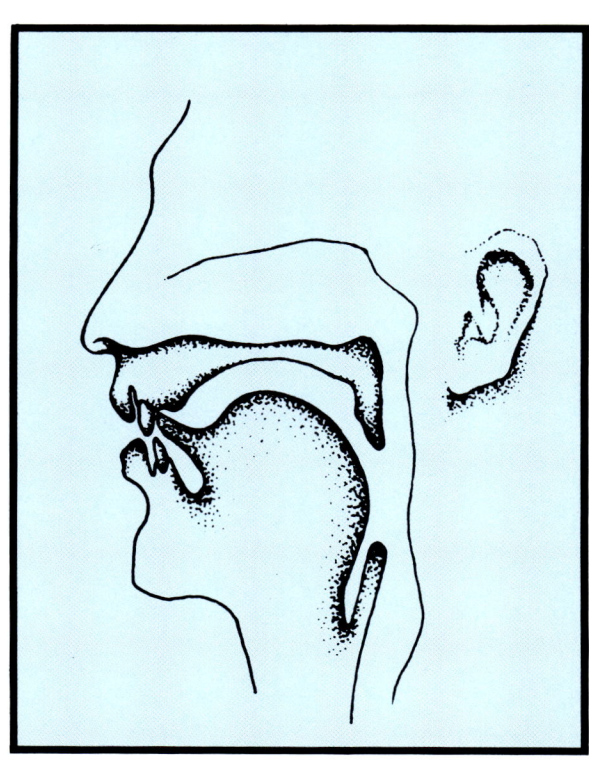

The position of the tongue for pronouncing the fricatives F and V. These sounds are made by allowing a breath-stream to escape through the narrow opening between the tongue and upper front teeth. The tongue is then released from this position to make the characteristic sound. V is voiced while F is voiceless.

The Letter M

M is a nasal consonant. In normal production the lips are brought together and breath is emitted through the nasal cavities. The lips are then parted and the consonant is complete. It has a singing quality dependent upon the nasal openings for the characteristic sound.

There are two prominent methods of transferring the action of the lips to the interior organs of the mouth. The first is to replace the lip action with the back of the tongue and soft velum. The back of the tongue is brought together with the soft velum and the M sound is made with tone being diverted through the nasal cavities. The tongue is then parted from the soft velum to complete the sound.

The second method is similar, except that the lip operation is

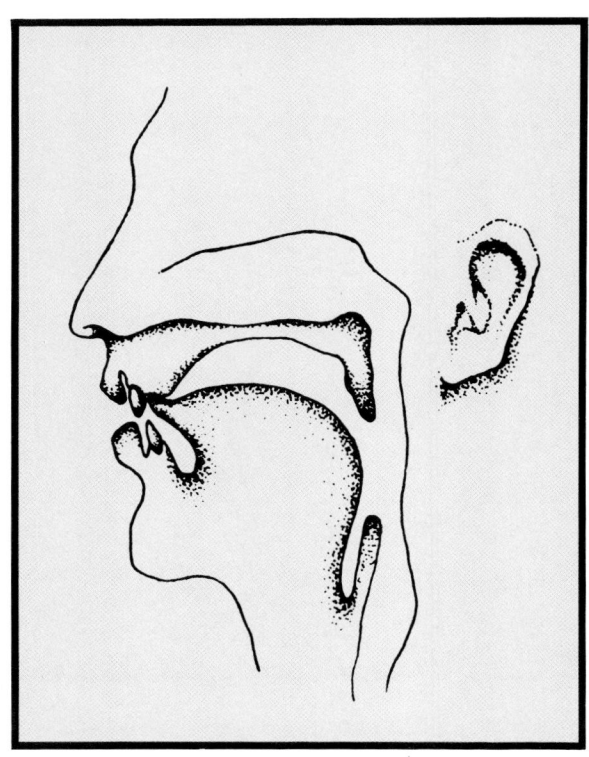

The position of the tongue for pronouncing the M consonant. The characteristic sound is made by diverting the tone through the nasal cavity before parting the tongue from this position.

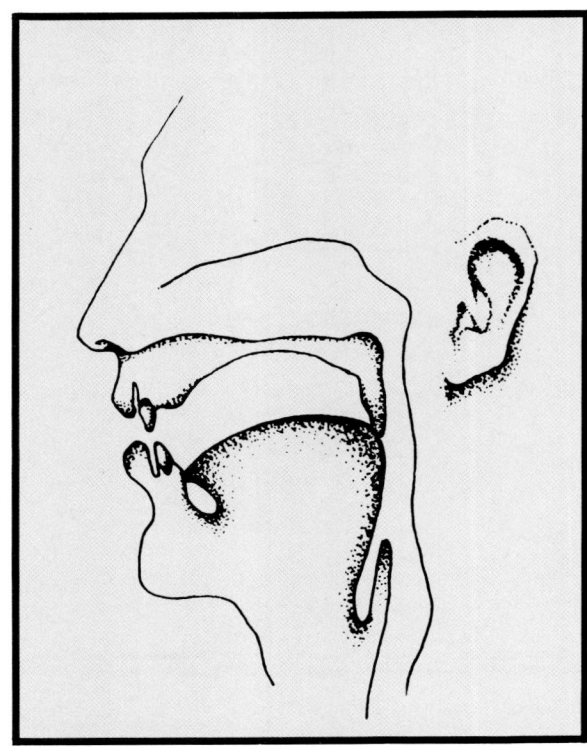

An alternative way of pronouncing the M consonant ventriloquially. The back of the tongue is brought into contact with the soft palate. The tone is diverted through the nasal cavity and the tongue is then released.

replaced with the tongue and the roof of the mouth. The edge of the tongue is pressed against the gum ridge so that the tip of the tongue is touching the upper front teeth. With the tongue in this position the M sound is made, diverting the tone through the nasal cavity and completed with the tongue parting from the gum ridge.

It may prove helpful at first to over-emphasize the nasal singing quality that precedes the parting of the tongue from the gum ridge (mm-money, mm-man, mm-mood, etc). It is this nasal characteristic that gives the M its distinctive sound.

The letter W

The last consonant to examine is W which is known as a glide. It is normally produced by the lips being brought together to form a round opening, with the back of the tongue being slightly elevated. In this position the vocal folds vibrate as the lips part to emit the voice sound.

Ventriloquially, W presents little difficulty, and it can easily be pronounced without lip movement. The duplication can be done by pronouncing it as the French word *oui*, permitting free use of the tongue without lip movement. However, there is a difference with words like where, white, and whale etc. that have a wh sound. For accurate pronunciation, care should be taken to distinguish between the W and the wh sounds.

When producing the ventriloquial voice the teeth and lips are kept slightly apart and it is important that the performer maintain a relaxed expression which should react naturally to the dialogue. A strained smile or staunch expression can be as distracting to the observer as movement of the lips. Performers should be able to change expression freely and naturally, listening to the ventriloquial voice as though it were the voice of someone talking to them. The expression smiling, serious, aloof, disgusted or whatever, should react accordingly, 'suit the action to the word'.

Lip control and clarity in pronouncing words ventriloquially can only be attained by constant practice. Certain exercises like the reading of newspapers or repeating phrases that contain difficult consonants will prove advantageous.

It is evident that the most valuable aid for the ventriloquist is the mirror. Daily practice in front of the mirror will soon reveal any shortcomings and help in their correction. The Great Lester had a small mirror installed into the mouth piece of the telephone he used during his performances. As he produced the ventriloquial voice, he would examine his lips in the mirror to ensure that there was no movement.

Distant voice ventriloquism

No phase of the art has excited more interest or created as much intrigue as distant voice ventriloquism. This is the technique that has given birth to the phrase 'throwing the voice', and has germinated the numerous anecdotes about ventriloquists practicing their skill on the unsuspecting.

For instance, in 1829, Gallanger was arrested in Dublin on suspicion of kidnapping when voices were heard coming from his trunk,[13] and Monsieur Charles once stopped the Staten Island ferry by calling in a distant voice 'man overboard'.[14] Present-day practitioners include Neville King, who constantly confuses hotel and airline staff with his invisible cat, and Clifford Guest, whose aerial voices bewilder passengers accompanying him in elevators.

Henry Cockton wrote *Adventures of Valentine Vox* after observing ventriloquists engaging in distant voice ventriloquism. Although Valentine Vox's superhuman power was fictitious, it was nonetheless based upon the vocal skill displayed by ventriloquists at that time. The most famous of these was Vattermare, whose expertise inspired Cockton's character. Like many performers at the time, Vattermare relied solely on distant voice technique and, during his entertainment, voices were heard coming from below the floor, on the roof, from trunks, bottles and various parts of the stage.

Today, the ventriloquial figure has become the focal point of the practice, making the art more visual, and distant voice ventriloquism is engaged to a lesser degree. Nonetheless, distant voice technique when mastered can prove a considerable asset to the performer and audiences universally respond to its display, recognizing it as a difficult and clever feat of ventriloquy.

The technique works as follows: When we produce normal speech sounds they are amplified by the mouth and nasal cavities which at the same time give the voice timbre and resonance. The loudness of these sounds is gauged by the proximity of the listener.

If one is placed outside a room to converse with someone inside, this natural amplification is not only suppressed by the distance, but the sounds are muffled as they become absorbed by the matter between the speaker and the listener. What reaches our ears in this case is the basic vocalization, without the full support of nature's resounding system. An example of this is heard when a phonograph record is played without connecting it to an amplifier. The sound is suppressed, having no timbre or resonance.

The principle of the distant voice is to imitate this basic vocalization. To attain this effect, the ventriloquist emits a vocal tone without allowing it the full benefit of the resounding system.

To do this, the lungs are filled with air and pressure is then exerted by the diaphragm and the impeded breath is slowly released over the vocal folds, confining the tone to the larynx area.

A similar action takes place when groaning, and this phase of the art has often been referred to as a cultivated groan. When we groan the stomach muscles aid the diaphragm in pushing the air from the lungs, and the tone is gradually squeezed out. It is useful to begin practicing the distant voice by making a groaning sound, and for this it is essential that the performer use the muscular breathing system as previously outlined.

Begin by filling the lungs with air, partially close the throat, then expel the air, gradually exerting pressure with the diaphragm while emiting a prolonged 'Ah' sound, confining the tone to the larynx. When this sound is mastered, try it with words and then with short phrases, noting that the greater the pressure applied on the vocal folds, the greater is the illusion of distance.

Because of the difficulty in phonating sounds with the distant voice, clarity is not easy and dialogue is usually kept to a minimum. Distant voice displays are often preceded by such phrases as, 'Can you hear me?' or 'Are you up there?', which are

Some animals produce a ventriloquial sound. This North American Pika emits a ventriloquial sound which seems to confuse its enemies as to its whereabouts.[15]

useful misdirectives. But to complete the illusion that these sounds are remote, great emphasis is placed upon the ability of the performer to misdirect the audience to the whereabouts of such sounds. This ability will depend on the artistry of the individual to act out the part with confidence and conviction.

Beginning distant voice technique, care should be taken not to practice too long, as undue strain may result in laryngeal problems. Like any new exercise of the body, practice should be kept to a minimum; one can gradually increase practice as the organs become accustomed to it.

While ventriloquism is an acquired practice, it rests with the individual to bring it to the level of an art form. This is not dependent upon mastering and perfecting the technique alone, or embellishing that technique with skilful dialogue and clever manipulation. Like every performing art, ventriloquism requires the indefinable talent of the individual to present it in such a way to arouse and excite the imagination of the audience. The ventriloquist must act out a dual role without appearing to act, creating with the illusion a sense of comedy and sometimes pathos.

These requisite skills are not easily acquired, and undoubtedly a ventriloquist's most effective teacher is the experience of performing in front of an audience. It is then, and only then, that the individual will begin to discover and develop potential and learn to master a performance, subtracting and adding to the repertoire until the result is a skilful and polished presentation.

Facing: A rare photograph of Edgar Bergen and Charlie McCarthy performing their 'Operation Sketch' in Sweden (1937).

Notes to Chapters

NOTES TO CHAPTER ONE

1. Thorndike, Lynn, *A History of Magic and Experimental Science* (London 1929), pp. 1-75.
2. Lucian of Samosata (125-190 A.D.), *The Works of Lucian*, Trans: A. M. Harmon (Mass 1936), Vol. 4, pp. 173-253.
3. Ibid., p. 211.
4. Rich, A., *A Dictionary of Greek and Roman Antiquities*, Vol. 21, p. 174 (London 1860). See also: Theodoret, Bishop of Cyrus (393-458 A.D.), *History of the Church*, Trans: Henry Bohn (London 1854).
5. Philostratus, Flavius (170-245 A.D.), *The Life of Appollonius of Tyana*, Trans: F. C. Conybeare (N.Y. 1921), Vol. 2, Bk. 4, Ch. 1, p. 31.
6. Gibson, W. B., *The Talking Idol* (U.S.A. 1922), pp. 17-19.
7. Breasted, James, *A History of Egypt* (N.Y. 1905), p. 348.
8. Hastings, James, *The Encyclopedia of Religion and Ethics* (N.Y. 1955), Vol. 4, pp. 775-830.
9. Cicero, Marcus Tullius (106-43, B.C.), *De Divinatone*, Trans: W. A. Falconer (London 1939), Bk. 2, p. 51.
10. *The Jewish Encyclopedia* (N.Y. 1905), Vol. 9, p. 204.
11. Driver, S.R., *A Critical and Exegetical Commentary on the Book of Deuteronomy* (U.S.A. 1909), pp. 224-226.
12. *Hebrew and English Lexicon of the Old Testament*, Trans: F. Brown, S. R. Driver, C. A. Briggs (London 1968), p. 15.
13. *The Babylonian Talmud*, English translation by I. Epstein (London 1978), Vol. 3, Sanhedrin 65a-65b, pp. 442-445.
14. Delitzch, F., *Biblical Commentary on the Prophecies of Isaiah*, Trans: J. Martin (Edinburgh 1873), Vol. 1, pp. 238-240.
15. Ibid.
16. Davies, W., *Magic and Divination Among the Hebrews and Their Neighbours* (London 1838), pp. 86-87.
17. Hofner, Harry A., "Second Millennium Antecedents to the Hebrew Ob," *The Journal of Biblical Literature* (U.S.A. 1967), Vol. 86, pp. 384-401.
18. Josephus, Flavius (38-93, A.D.), *Jewish Antiquities*, Trans: J. Thackeray, R. Marcus (Mass 1934), gr/eng, Vol. 6, pp. 330-339.
19. *The Septuagint with Apocrypha: Greek and English*, Zondervan edition (U.S.A. 1985), pp. 395-396. I Sam. 28:3-9. See also: Patristic Lexicon, Edited by G. Lamp (London 1961), p. 397.
20. Alciphron (2nd century A.D.), *Letters of Courtesans*, Trans: A. Benner, F. Fobes (London 1912), Vol. 1, Bk. 4, 19, 15, pp. 334-335.
21. Hippocrates (400 B.C.), *Book on Common Diseases*, Bk. 5.

22. Plato (427-348 B.C.), *The Sophist,* Trans: H. Fowler (Mass 1952), pp. 397-399.
23. Photius (820-891), *Patrologia Graeca,* J.P. Migne, Vol. 103, pp. 3-75b.
24. Aristophanes (450-388 B.C.), *Wasps,* Trans: B. B. Rogers (Mass 1960), 1019, pp. 504-505.
25. Loewe, M., Blacker, C., *Oracles and Divination,* (U.S.A. 1936), pp. 376-377.
26. Plutarch (46-120 A.D.), *Moralia (De Oraculo-Defecto),* Trans: F. Babbitt (Mass 1936), pp. 376-377.
27. Sophocles (495-406 B.C.), *The Fragments of Sophocles,* A. C. Pearson (U.K. 1917), Vol. 1, p. 37 (Fr 59).
28. Fowler, W., *The Religious Experience of the Roman People* (London 1911), p. 307.
29. *The New Testament Octapla,* Edited by L. A. Weigle (N.Y. 1962), Acts 16:16, pp. 756-757. See also: *The New Testament from 26 translations,* Zondervan ed. (U.S.A. 1967), pp. 542-543.
30. Augustine, St. of Hippo (354-430 A.D.), *De Doctra Chris,* Ed: M. Dods, Vol. 9, Bk. 9, Ch. 24, p. 60. See also: *The Biblical Illustrator,* The Acts, J. Exell (U.S.A. 1954), Vol. 11, pp. 498-499.
31. Tertullian, Quintus, Septimus, Florens (160-230 A.D.), *Adversus Marcionem,* Trans: E. Evans (London 1972), Bk. 4, 25, 4, pp. 398-399.
32. Clement, St. Titus, Flavius (150-215 A.D.), *Exhortation to the Greeks,* Trans: G. W. Butterworth (London 1939), Ch. 2, pp. 28-29.
33. Origin, Adamantius (185-254 A.D.), Op. cit. (see note 23 above), *De Engastrimytho,* Vol. 9, 490-498.
34. Gregory, St. of Nyssa (330-395 A.D.), *De Pythonissa,* Ibid., Vol. 45, Col. 107-114.
35. Eustathius, St. of Antioch (270-360 A.D.), *De Engastrimytho contra Originem,* Ibid., Vol. 18, Col. 613-674.
36. Clement, St., *The Instructor,* Trans: A. Roberts (U.S.A. 1885), p. 241
37. Op. cit., see note 2 above. *Lexiphanes,* Vol. 5, pp. 320-321.
38. Tylor, E. B., *Primitive Cultures* (London 1929), pp. 121-123.
39. Ibid.
40. Doolittle, J., *Social Life of the Chinese* (U.S.A. 1865), pp. 441-442.
41. Callaway, Henry, *Religion of the Amazula* (London 1870), p. 362.

42. Lyon, Edward, *Private Journal of Captain Edward Lyon* (London 1824), pp. 358-360.

NOTES TO CHAPTER TWO

1. Photius (820-891), *151 Epistle,* Op, cit. (see Chapter 1 note 23), Vol. 101, Col. 553-554.
2. Fisher, G. P., *History of the Christian Church* (N.Y. 1889), p. 88.
3. Nicole Oresme, Bishop of Lisieux (1320-1382), *De Configurationibus Qualitatium,* Trans: M. Clagett (Wisconsin 1916), Part 2, pp. 337-371.
4. Neame, Alan, *The Holy Maid of Kent* (London 1971), pp. 335-336.
5. Cranmer, Thomas, Archbishop of Canterbury (1489-1556), Letter to Archdeacon Hawings, dated December 20, 1533; See Remains of Thomas Cranmer, H. Jenkyns (London 1833), Letter number 84.
6. Scot, Reginald (1538-1599), *Discovery of Witchcraft* (1584), Bk. 7, Ch. 1-3.
7. Ibid.
8. Hopkins, Matthew (-d 1647), *Discovery of Witches* (1647).
9. Robbins, R. H., *The Encyclopedia of Witchcraft and Demonology* (N.Y. 1959), pp. 190-191.
10. James I, *Demonology* (1597).
11. Eugubinus (Steuchus) Augustus (1496-1549), *Recognitio Vateris Testements ad Hebraicam* (Italy 1529), Ch. 19, pp. 139-140.
12. Allatius, Leo (1586-1669), *De Engastrimytho Syntagma, De Engastrimytho Dissertatio* (Italy 1661), p. 1053.
13. Brodeau, Jean (1500-1563), See *Lampas sive fax artium liberalium,* Janus Gruterus (Italy 1604), Vol. 4, pp. 72-73.
14. Ibid.
15. Tallemant, Gedeon, Reaux, des. (1619-1692), *Les Historiettes de Tallemant des Reaux* (Paris 1862), pp. 99-102.
16. Dickinson, Edmund (1624-1707), *Delphi Phoeicizantos* (Oxford 1655), pp. 81-82.
17. Ady, Thomas, *A Candle in the Dark* (London 1656).
18. See note 12 above. See also: *The Religious Encyclopedia, Schaff-Herzog* (U.S.A. 1960), Vol. 1, p. 129.
19. Garmann, G. F., *De miraculis mortuorum* (Lipsic 1709), p. 405.
20. Blount, Thomas, *Glossographia* (London 1688), pp. 681-682.
21. Casserius, Julius (1552-1616), *De Vocis Auditusque Organis Historia Anatomia* (Italy 1601), p. 172.

22. Digby, Sir Kenelm (1603-1665), *The Nature of Bodies* (England 1645).
23. Amman, Conrad (1669-1724), *De Loquela* (Holland 1700). See *Dissertation on Speech* (London 1873), p. 131.
24. Van Dale, Anthony (1638-1708), *Idolatry and Superstitions* (Holland 1690), p. 652. See also: Bekker, Balthazar, *De Betovorde Weereld* (Holland 1691), Bk. 2, Ch. 4, pp. 74-75.
25. Labat, Jean Baptiste (1663-1738), *Noveau Voyage aux Iles Francaises de l'America* (Paris 1722), Vol. 2, pp. 64-65.

NOTES TO CHAPTER 3
1. Byrom, John, *The Private Remains of John Byrom* (London 1857), p. 116.
2. *Gentleman's Magazine* (London 1773), pp. 437-484.
3. Pinks, William, *The History of Clerkenwell* (London 1881), pp. 276-279.
4. Hawkins, John, *History of Music* (London 1776), p. 788.
5. *Pantologia Cylopaedia* (London 1813), see Ventriloquism.
6. Caulfield, James, *Portraits, Memoirs and Characters of Remarkable Persons* (London 1813), pp. 75-75.
7. *Daily Post* (London), April 24, 1722.
8. Professor Lee, *Boys Own Paper* (London 1881), Vol. 3, pp. 373.
9. See note 6 above, p. 375.
10. See note 8 above
11. Wheatley, Henry, *Hogarth's London* (London 1909), p. 175.
12. Chapelle, Abbe de la (1710-1792), *Le Ventriloque ou L'Engastrimthe* (London 1772), p. 80.
13. Ibid., p. 112.
14. Ibid., p. 12.
15. Ibid., p. 87.

NOTES TO CHAPTER 4
1. See note 8, chapter 3.
2. *Thoronton's: History of Nottinghamshire* (London 1797), Vol. 2, p. 149.
3. Shaw, S., *History of Staffordshire* (London 1801), Vol. 1, p. 75.
4. *The Oracle and Public Advertiser* (London), August 31, 1796.
5. Ibid., August 17, 1796.
6. *The Times* (London), June 28, 1797.
7. Richerand, A., *Elements in Physiology*, Trans: G. Delys (London 1829), p. 446.

8. Comte, Appollinaire, Christien, Emmanuel, *Voyages et Seances Anecdotiques de Comte* (Paris 1816).
9. See note 8, chapter 3, p. 406.
10. Eastman, J. R., *History of Andover, New Hampshire* (U.S.A. 1910), pp. 425-426.
11. *The Columbian Centennial Federalist,* June 14, 1804.
12. Saxe, John Godfrey, *The Poetical Works of John Godfrey Saxe* (New York 1892), pp. 64-65.
13. *Gleason's Pictorial Drawing Room Companion* (Boston), May 15, 1852.
14. Moncreiff, William, *Adventures of a Ventriloquist, or The Rogueries of Nicholas as Embodied by Mons Alexandre* (London 1822).
15. *The Edinburgh Advertiser,* April 30, 1824, Poem dated April 23.
16. Waldin, H. G., *The Public Library of the City of Boston* (Boston 1911), pp. 1-61.
17. Winsor, J., *The Memorial History of Boston* (Boston 1881), Vol. 4, pp. 284-286. See also: *More Books, the Bulletin of the Boston Public Library* (1927), Vol. 2, no. 8.
18. *The Morning Chronicle,* June 8, 1840. See also: *Magic Magazine* (London 1903), p. 46.
19. Sutton, George, *A Treatise on Ventriloquism* (U.S.A. 1833).

NOTES TO CHAPTER 5

1. Cockton, Henry, *The Life and Adventures of Valentine Vox the Ventriloquist* (London 1840).
2. *The Dictionary of National Biography,* Vol. 4, p. 658.
3. Ibid., Vol. 12, p. 161. See also: *The London Journal and Weekly Record of Literature, Science and Art,* March 17, 1849.
4. *The London Illustrated News,* January 27, 1855.
5. *The Standard,* March 2, 1849.
6. *The London Entr'acte,* December 17, 1898.
7. Jester, G. W., *Ventriloquism and the Art of Imitation* (1880).
8. Smith, George, *Memoirs and Anecdotes of Mr. Love* (London 1875).
9. *The Sphinx,* October 1932, p. 301.
10. Price, David, *Magic* (N.Y. 1910), pp. 55-57.
11. *The Amusement World,* May 1874.
12. *The Era,* April 16, 1871.
13. Ibid., February 8, 1874.
14. *Encore,* January 12, 1874.
15. Ibid., February 17, 1893.

16. Ibid., November 10, 1893.
17. *Variety Theatre,* November 17, 1905.
18. *Strand Magazine,* 1897, Vol. 8, p. 416.
19. See note 14 above.
20. *Grapevine News,* December 1948.
21. *Variety Theatre,* June 30, 1905.
22. *The Stage and Foyer,* February 1926.

NOTES TO CHAPTER 6
1. *Encore,* July 10, 1902.
2. *The London Times,* October 15, 1957.
3. *The Performer,* December 1946.
4. *Encore,* July 25, 1906.
5. *Encore,* November 21, 1920.
6. Prince, Don, *Reflections in a Glass Eye* (California 1960), p. 21.
7. *The Pilot Comic,* 1936.
8. *The London Times,* April 15, 1948.
9. *Encore,* July 24, 1911.
10. Ibid., December 25, 1928.
11. Ibid., September 14, 1920.
12. Ibid., March 13, 1913.
13. Ibid., February 16, 1905.
14. *The Oracle,* Vol. 17, no. 21.
15. Ibid.
16. Ibid., Vol. 15, no. 5.
17. Green, Abel, Laurie, Joe, *Show Biz from Vaude to Video* (New York, 1951), pp. 271-273.
18. *The Oracle,* December 1950.
19. *The New York Times Film Review,* September 14, 1929.
20. Ibid., August 3, 1925.

NOTES TO CHAPTER 7
1. *Encore,* March 17, 1927.
2. *Colliers,* April 29, 1950.
3. Bergen, Candice, *Knock Wood* (N.Y. 1984), pp. 19-34.
4. See note 2 above.
5. *Colliers,* March 20, 1937.
6. Author's Interview
7. *Time,* November 20, 1944.
8. See note 5 above.
9. *Reader's Digest,* March 1941.
10. See note 2 above.
11. See note 7 above.

12. The Bergen and McCarthy duo appeared in twelve shorts for Vitaphone from 1930 to 1936. Feature movies were as follows: *The Goldwyn Follies* (1938), *Letter of Introduction* (1938), *You Can't Cheat an Honest Man* (1939), *Charlie McCarthy Detective* (1939), *Look Who's Laughing* (1941), *Here We Go Again* (1942), *Stage Door Canteen* (1943), *Song of the Open Road* (1944), *Fun and Fancy Free* (1947), *The Muppet Movie* (1979).
13. *Newsweek,* July 17, 1937.
14. See note 7 above.
15. *Time,* August 8, 1944.
16. See note 2 above.
17. *Chicago Tribune,* September 22, 1978.
18. *Reader's Digest,* October 1984.
19. Op. cit. (see Chapter 6, note 19), June 29, 1946.
20. Brough, Peter, *Educating Archie* (London 1955).
21. Ibid., pp. 39-40.
22. Ibid., p. 42.
23. Ibid., p. 41.
24. Ibid., p. 67.
25. Ibid., p. 98.
26. Ibid., pp. 120-122.
27. Ibid., p. 123.
28. Ibid., p. 149.

NOTES TO CHAPTER 8

1. Op. cit. (see Chapter 3, note 12), p. 93.
2. Ibid., p. 89.
3. See note 16, chapter 5.
4. Public Records Office, *patent for compressed air system of working figures,* No. 21, 877, December 1893.
5. Ibid., *Patent for improvements in ventriloquial apparatus,* No. 27, 720, 1907.
6. *Double Talk* (U.S.A. 1937-38).
7. *Lemare* catalogue (U.K. 1930).
8. *Saturday Evening Post,* July 20, 1946.
9. *Moonbeams* 1965
10. *The Standard,* October 7, 1932.
11. *South Londoner,* November 10, 1971.
12. *Saturday Evening Post,* May 9, 1954.
13. Op. cit., see note 20, ch. 7, p. 118.
14. *American Weekly,* October 1937.
15. Adams, Joey, *From Gags to Riches,* (N.Y. 1946).
16. Op. cit., See note 6, Chap. 6, pp. 164-166.

17. *The Courier Journal Magazine,* January 6, 1957. See also: *The Atlantic Monthly,* August 1989.
18. *The Oracle,* 1950-1960 (U.S.A.).
19. *Grapevine News,* 1941-1950.
20. *Ventogram,* 1963-1970.
21. See note 8 above.
22. *Co-op Zeitung,* No. 34, August 24, 1989 (Switzerland).
23. Maccabe, Fredrick, *The Art of Ventriloquism* (London 1875), p. 79.

NOTES TO CHAPTER 9

1. Ross, Gordon, *Television Jubilee,* (London 1961), p. 14.
1a. *Your Health,* April 23, 1985.
2. *Radio Times,* November 1936.
3. *Times Magazine* (London 1978)
4. *The T.V. Whirligig* (London 1950)
5. *The People Magazine* (London), April 22, 1990.
6. *The Complete Directory to Prime Time T.V. Shows* (U.S.A. 1981), p. 224.
7. Op. cit., see note 12, chapter 8.
8. *The London Times,* November 17, 1964.
9. *Life Magazine,* December 22, 1958.
10. See note 6 above, p. 585.
11. *Look Magazine,* July 12, 1955.
12. *Los Angeles Times,* February 20, 1989.
13. *Newsweek,* December 4, 1950.
14. Op. cit., see note 12, chapter 8.
15. Guest, Clifford, *Comprehensive Course in Ventriloquism.*
16. See note 6, above, p. 393.
17. *Ebony,* October 1981.
18. *People's Magazine,* May 23, 1983.
19. *The London Times,* October 3, 1950.
20. *The Disney Magazine,* April 24, 1988.
21. Balder, Eugene, *De Ventriloquia* (Madrid 1915).
22. See note 7, chapter 7.
23. *Time Magazine,* December 25, 1978.
24. See note 18, chapter 7.
25. *Der Kladdadast,* October 1881.

NOTES TO CHAPTER 10

1. Op. cit., see note 12, chapter 5.
2. Puck Comic, *Val Fox, Boy Ventriloquist and Detective* (1914). Wonder Comic, *Merry Mick the Boy Ventriloquist* (1942).
3. Op. cit., see note 3, chapter 5.

4. Pinchbeck, W.F., *The Expositor or, Many Mysteries Unravelled* (Boston 1805).
5. Op. cit., see note 12, chapter 8.
6. Op. cit., see note 19, chapter 4, p. 32.
7. Bergen, Edgar, *How to Become a Ventriloquist* (U.S.A. 1938), p. 14.
8. Op. cit., see note 20, chapter 7, p. 42.
9. Op. cit., see note 4, chapter 4.
10. Op. cit., see note 23, chapter 8.
11. Op. cit., see note 19, chapter 4, p. 30.
12. Prince, Arthur, *The Whole Art of Ventriloquism* (London 1915), p. 9.
13. *The Edinburgh and Evening Courant*, December 14, 1829.
14. *The New Hampshire Patriot and State Gazette*, February 8, 1820.
15. Orr, Robert, *The Little Known Pika* (N.Y. 1908).

Bibliography

Adams, Joey
From Gags to Riches (N.Y. 1946)

Ady, Thomas
A Candle in the Dark (London 1656)

Allatius, Leo
De Engastrimytho Syntagma, De Engastrimytho Dissertatio (Italy 1661)

Alciphron
Letters of Courtesans. Trans: A. Benner, F. Fobes. 'Loeb Series' (London 1912)

Amman, Conrad
De Loquela (Holland 1700)

Aristophanes
Wasps. Trans: B.B. Rogers. 'Loeb Series' (Mass 1960)

Augustine, St.
The Works of St. Augustine (De Doctra Chris). Ed: Marcus Dods. Vol. 9, bk. 2, p. 60. See Excell

Bekker, Balthazer
De Betovorde Weereld (Holland 1691)

Bergen, Candice
Knock Wood (N.Y. 1984)

Bergen, Edgar
How to Become a Ventriloquist (U.S.A. 1938)

Blount, Thomas
Glossographia (London 1688)

Breasted, James
A History of Egypt (N.Y. 1905)

Brodeau, Jean
Lampas Sive Fax Syntagma Liberalium, Janus Gruterus (Italy 1604)

Brough, Peter
Educating Archie (London 1955)

Brown, F., Driver, S.R., Briggs, C.A.
Hebrew and English Lexicon of the Old Testament (London 1968)

Byrom, John
The Private Remains of John Byrom (London 1857)

Callaway, H.
Religions of the Amazula (London 1870)

Casserius, Julius
De Vocis Auditusque Organis Historia Anatomia (Italy 1601)

Chapelle, Abbe de la
Le Ventriloque ou L'Engastrimthe (London 1772)

Cicero, Marcus Tullius
De Divinatone. Trans: W.A. Falconer. 'Loeb Series' (London 1939)

Clement, St.
Exhortation to the Greeks. Trans: G.W. Butterworth (London 1939)

Cockton, Henry
The Life and Adventures of Valentine Vox the Ventriloquist (London 1840)

Comte, A.E.C.
Voyages et Seances Anecdotiques de Comte (Paris 1816)

Cranmer, Thomas
Remains of Thomas Cranmer, H. Jenkyns (London 1833)

Davies, W.
Magic and Divination among the Hebrews and their Neighbours (London 1838)

Delitzch, F.
Biblical Commentary on the Prophecies of Isaiah. Trans: J. Martin (Edinburgh 1873)

Dickinson, Edmund
Delphi Phoeicizantos (Oxford 1655)

Digby, Kenelm
The Nature of Bodies (England 1645)

Doolittle, J.
Social Life of the Chinese (U.S.A. 1865)

Driver, S.R.
A Critical and Exegetical Commentary on the Book of Deuteronomy (N.Y. 1909)

Eastman, J.R.
History of Andover, New Hampshire (U.S.A. 1910)

Eugubinus, (Steuchus) Augustus
Recognitio Vateris Testements ad Hebraicam (Italy 1604)

Eustathius, St. of Antioch
De Engastrimthyo Contra Originem. J.P. Migne, Patrologia Greaca. Vol. 18.

Excell, J.
The Biblical Illustrator (N.Y. 1954)

Fisher, G.P.
History of the Christian Church (N.Y. 1889)

Fowler, W.
The Religious Experience of the Roman People (London 1911)

Garmann, G.F.
De Miraculis Mortuorum (Lipsic 1709)

Gibson, W.B.
The Talking Idol (U.S.A. 1922)

Green, A., Laurie, J.
Show Biz from Vaud to Video (N.Y. 1951)

Gregory, St. of Nyssa
De Pythonissa. J.P. Migne. Patrologia Graeca. Vol. 45.

Guest, Clifford
Comprehensive Course in Ventriloquism (Melbourne 1966)

Hastings, James
The Encyclopedia of Religion and Ethics (N.Y. 1955)

Hippocrates
Epidemics, bk. 5

Hofner, H.R.
(Second Millennium Antecedents to the Hebrew Ob.) Journal of Biblical Literature (U.S.A. 1967)

Hopkins, Matthew
Discovery of Witches (England 1647)

James I
Demonology (1597)

Jester, G.W.
Ventriloquism and the Art of Imitation (1880)

Jewish Encyclopedia
The Jewish Encyclopedia (N.Y. 1905)

Josephus Flavius
Jewish Antiquities. Trans: J. Thackeray, R. Marcus. 'Loeb Series' (Mass 1934)

Labat, Jean Baptiste
Noveau Voyage aux Iles Francaises de L'America (Paris 1722)

Loewe, M., Blacker, C.
Oracles and Divination (Colorado 1981)

Lucian of Samosata
The Works of Lucian. Vol. 4-5. Trans: A.M. Harmon. 'Loeb Series' (Mass 1936)

Lyon, E.
Private Journal of Captain Edward Lyon (London 1824)

Maccabe, Fredrick
The Art of Ventriloquism (London 1875)

Migne, Jacques Paul
Patrologiae Cursus Completus (Paris 1878)

National Biography
The National Biography (London)

Neame, A.
The Holy Maid of Kent (London 1971)

New Testament
The New Testament Octapla. Ed: L.A. Weigle (N.Y. 1962)

Oreseme, Nicole
De Configurationibus Qualitatium. Trans: M. Clagett (Wisc 1916)

Origin, Adamantius
De Engastrimytho. J.P. Migne, Patrologia Graeca. Vol. 12.

Pantologia Cyclopedia
The Pantologia Cyclopedia (London 1813)

Patristic Lexicon
The Patristic Lexicon. Ed: G. Lamp (London 1961)

Philostratus, Flavius
The Life of Appollonius of Tyana. Vol. 2. Trans: F.C. Conybeare. 'Loeb Series' (N.Y. 1921)

Photius
J.P. Migne. *Patrologia Greaca.* Vol. I.

Pinchbeck, W.F.
The Expositor or, Many Mysteries Unravelled (Boston 1805)

Pinks, William
History of Clerkenwell (London 1881)

Plato
The Sophist. Trans: H. Fowler. 'Loeb Series' (Mass 1952)

Plutarch
Moralia. Trans: F. Babbitt. 'Loeb Series' (Mass 1936)

Price, D.
Magic (N.Y. 1910)

Prince, Arthur
The Whole Art of Ventriloquism (London 1915)

Prince, Don
Reflections in a Glass Eye (California 1960)

Rich, A.
A Dictionary of Greek and Roman Antiquities (London 1860)

Richerand, A.
Elements in Physiology. Trans: G. Delys (London 1829)

Robbins, R.H.
The Encyclopedia of Witchcraft and Demonology (N.Y. 1959)

Ross, G.
Television Jubilee, The Story of 25 Years of B.B.C. (London 1961)

Saxe, John Godfrey
The Poetical Works of John Godfrey Saxe (N.Y. 1892)

Scot, Reginald
Discovery of Witchcraft (1584)

Septuagint
Septuagint with Apocrypha, Greek and English (U.S.A. 1985)

Shaw, S.
History of Staffordshire (London 1801)

Sophocles
The Fragments of Sophocles. A.C. Pearson (London 1917)

Sutton, George
A Treatise on Ventriloquism (U.S.A. 1833)

Tallemant, G.R.
Les Historiettes de Tallement des Reaux (Paris 1862)

Talmud
The Babylonian Talmud. Trans: I. Epstein (London 1978)

Tertullian, Quintus, Septimus
Adversus Marcionem. Trans: E. Evans. 'Loeb Series.' (London 1972)

Theodoret
History of the Church. Trans: Henry Bohn (London 1854)

Thorndike, Lynn
The History of Magic and Experimental Science (London 1929)

Thoronton
Thoronton's History of Nottinghamshire (London 1797)

Tylor, E.B.
Primitive Cultures (London 1929)

Van Dale, Anthony
Idolatry and Superstitions (Holland 1690)

Waldin, H.G.
The Public Library of the City of Boston (Mass 1911)

Wheatley, Henry
Hogarth's London (London 1909)

Winsor, Justin
The Memorial History of Boston (Mass 1881)

Ventriloquist Magazines

Breezes
Chicago 1940, mimeographed
George 'Pinxy' Larsen

Dialogue
The Ventriloquist World Association
New Jersey 1986-

Grapevine News
International Brotherhood of Ventriloquists
Illinois 1941-1950

The New Vent-O-Gram
International Ventriloquists Association
Illinois 1970-1984   (successor to the *Vent-O-Gram*)

Newsy Vents
North American Association of Ventriloquism
Colorado 1945-1973, mimeographed, printed 1973-

The New Oracle
Society of American Ventriloquists
Baltimore 1976-1986   (successor to the *Oracle*)

The Oracle
International Brotherhood of Ventriloquists
Kentucky 1950-1960   (successor to the *Grapevine News*)

Vent-O-Gram
San Francisco 1963-1968, mimeographed
Dec. 1968-1969, printed

The Ventriloquist Guild Journal
The Ventriloquist Guild
Chicago 1986-   (preceded by the 'Lester Letter')

Vent News
Chicago 1972
Izzi Rizzy

Information

The Ventriloquists World Association
103 Ironwood Court, Vinton, Virginia 24179-4923

National Association of American Ventriloquists
Box 420, Littleton, Colorado 80120

The Ventriloquist Guild
Box 203, Kenilworth, Illinois 60043

Museum of Ventriloquism (Museum Der Bauchrednerkunst)
Hauptgasse 81, CH 9113 Degersheim, Switzerland

Vent Haven Museum, Inc.
33 Maple Avenue, Ft. Mitchell, Covington, Kentucky 41011

Acknowledgements

I would like to express my appreciation to the following individuals, libraries and museums who have helped in the preparation of this work.

Harry Price Library, London University, particularly Mr. Wesencroft, without whose initial help this work would not have been possible.

British Museum; Colindale Newspaper Library; Society of Ancient and Hellenic Studies; Dr. Williams Library; London Bible College; City of Westminster Library; Public Records Office; Victoria and Albert Museum; The Science Museum, Kensington; John Soan Museum; National Portrait Gallery; British Film Institute; Mander and Mitcheson Collection; BBC Archives; British Music Hall Society; Nottingham Public Library; Walter Scott Library, Abbotsford; Biblioteca Apostolica Vaticana; Oferreinchitche Nationalbibliothek, Austria.

My thanks to the following libraries and organisations in the USA. Carnegie Library of Pittsburg; Boston Public Library; Harvard Theatre Collection; Library of Congress; New York Public Library; New Hampshire Public Library; Vent Haven Museum Inc., particularly Susan Defalaise; Metropolitan Library of Toronto, Canada; University College of Los Angeles; Los Angeles Public Library.

Thanks to Dennis Alwood for additional information concerning Edgar Bergen.

For the translations from Latin I wish to thank James Morrison, and for the translations from German, Perviz Pavri.

Picture Credits

The author gratefully acknowledges the following organizations and individuals for permission to reproduce copyright illustrations.

Jacket, Coca Cola Company, The Bergen Foundation
31 Kent Public Library
30, 34 Trustees of the National Gallery, London
38 Apostolica Vatican, Rome
44-45 Bridgeman Art Library Ltd.
61 Dover Publications
108 Joseph E. Levine Presents, Inc.
111 Gala Films Ltd. (Devil Doll)
112-125 The Bergen Foundation
116 Time/Warner Magazine Inc. (Copyright 1944)
120 Coca Cola Company
124 United States Postal Service
125 Walt Disney Productions
107 Coca Cola Company
130-133 British Broadcasting Corporation
142, 145 Bill Nelson Inc.
149 David Erskine
150 The Courier Journal and Louisville Times
175 Henson Associates Inc. (1980)
178 Columbia Pictures Television (Soap)
179 Johnny Hart Inc.
194 Punch Magazine
208 Dennis Alwood

Special thanks to the ventriloquial artists who supplied photographs of themselves for this work.
All other illustrations from the Valentine Vox Ventriloquial Collection, housed at the Museum der Bauchrednerkunst, Switzerland.

Index

A

Acrobats, 55
Actors, 20
Acts of Apostles, 22
Adelphi Theatre, 63
Adlington, 30
Adversus Marionem, 23
Africa, 26
Alan, Ray 144, 167
Alba, 13
AlexanderPalace, 165
Alexander of Abonoteichus, 11, 13
Alexandre, Mons, 62-68
Allatius, Leo, 38
Alwood, Dennis, 143
Ameche, Don, 116
America, 59-60, 67, 68, 72, 76, 80, 99, 113, 114, 122, 141, 152, 168
Amman, Conrad, 38-39
Anatomical History of the Voice and Speaking Organs, 38
Anderson, Prof, 75
Andrews, Archie, 127-133, 144, 145, 147, 187
Andrews, Julie, 130-132
Anthroposcopy, 14
Apollo, 20
Apollonius, 13
Aristophanes, 18
Askins, Joseph, 55-58, 188
Assembly Rooms, 72
Astor, A. C., 87, 96, 167
Astrology, 14
Augurs, 23
Augustine, St, 23, 24
Automaton, 69, 76, 143
Autophone, 13

B

"B" 190-191
Baal-obh, 16
Baird, John, Logie, 165-166
Balaban & Katz Theatre, 101
Balder, Eugenio, 174-177
Balomancy, 14
Bartholomews Fair, 44, 45, 47, 49
Barton, Elizabeth, 30, 31
B.B.C., 128, 167, 168
Belly-demon, 24
Belly-prophets, 18
Belly-speakers, 18
Benny, Jack, 124
Bergen, Candice, 174, 177
Bergen, Edgar, 112-126, 127, 128, 130, 133, 140, 151, 168, 170, 175, 177, 184, 187
Berger, W.S., 150, 152
Berlin, Walter & Gregory, 152
Bick, James, 44, 47
Blaskett, Ron, 135
Blizt, Signor, 76
Blount's dictionary, 38
Boleyn, Anne, 30
Boston Public Library, 67, 68
Brabant, Louis, 34-35
Brighton, Herbert, 41, 107, 144
Britten, Thomas, 41-43
Broadway Eddy, 184
Brodeau, Jean, 34
Brough, Arthur, 126
Brough Peter, 127-133, 144, 171, 187
Brown, Charlie 151, 169
Burns, James, 53-55
Bygraves, Max, 130, 132
Byrom, John, 41
Byron, Jr, Frank, 100-101, 152, 184

C

Caeser, Augustus, 22
Caesers Palace, 124
Carmen, Mary, 177
Casserius, Julius, 38, 39
Catholic, 30
Cato, 14
Cavalcanti, 126
Cavanagh, Peter, 128
Chandler, Claude, 138
Chaney, Lon, 107, 108
Chapelle, Abbe de la, 50-51, 136
Charing Cross Theatre, 75
Charlie McCarthy Detective, 121
Charles, Mons, 194
Chase and Sanbourne Hour, 116
Chautauqua Circuit, 114, 115
Cheiromancy, 14, 19
China, 13
Chirgwin, 105
Christian, 23, 24, 30
Christianity, 22
Clairvoyancy, 30
Clark, Elizabeth, 34
Clark, Johnson, 96, 99, 167
Cledonomancy, 14
Clement, St, 23, 24
Clinch, John, 47
Clowns, 44
Coca Cola, 120
Cockton, Henry, 71, 72, 194
Collet, Mons, 36
Colin, Sid, 130
Cole, Walter, 78-80, 139, 179, 181, 188

Comte, L. C. E., 58, 59
Comu, Mons, 34
Consonants, 189-192
Constantine, 29
Constantinople, 29
Cooper, John, 99, 101
Coram, 92-94, 139, 144, 151, 153, 179
Coster Joe, 87-89, 139, 151
Coudrill, Francis, 167
Coward, Noel, 116
Cramner, Thomas, 30
Cromwell, Oliver, 59
Crystal Palace, 88
Curtis-Dustin, V., 119

D

Daisy May, 166, 167
D'Albert, 138, 144
Davies, Alex, 71
Davies, E. D., 77, 79, 153, 188
Dead of Night, 111, 126
De Engastrimthyo Syntagma, 38
De Engastrimthyo Dessertatio, 38
De Loquela, 39
De Lion, Mrs. Clement, 103
Delphi, 20, 21
Demon, 24
Demonic, 21, 25, 38
Demonology, 29
De Oraculo Defecto, 21
De Pythones, 24
Deuteronomy, 16
Devil Doll, 111
Dexter, Herbert, 147, 150
Diabolical, 29, 33
Diaphram, 185, 186
Digby, Sir Kenelm, 39
Dinsdale, Shirley, 171
Discoverie of Witchcraft, 32, 33, 35
Distant voice, 76, 80, 184, 194, 195
Divination, 14, 16, 18, 21, 29, 33, 34
Diviners, 14, 15, 18, 19, 21, 22, 24, 25, 26
Dolls, 25, 26, 49, 50, 54, 55, 76, 80, 120, 136, 137, 153
Donskaji, Mary & Jane, 174
Double Talk, 140
Do You Trust Your Wife, 171
Dreams, Lydia, 102, 103, 104, 105, 153
Dummy, 87, 126, 127, 135, 147
Duncan, O.A., 85

E

EducatingArchie, 130, 131, 142, 147, 171
Edwards, Maude 96, 102, 103
Edwards, Tom, 96-98

Egypt, 14, 18
Egyption Hall, 75
Endor, Witch of, 16, 17, 18, 23, 24, 29, 30, 38
Erasmus, 37
Eskimo, 27
Esquire Magazine, 116
Etruscans, 22
Eugubinus, Augustine, 33
Eurycleis, 18, 20, 21
Eurycles, 18, 20, 21, 27
Eustathius, St, 24, 38
Everty, Eric, 153
Evocation, 16, 21

F

"F" 190, 191
Fairfax, Beatrix, 119
Familiar, 16, 22, 25, 26, 33, 34, 39, 56, 135, 139, 170, 175
Fannigus, 37
Farfel, 148, 171
Felix, Geoff, 137
Fields, W.C., 118, 119, 120
Figure, 10, 11, 25, 41, 54, 63, 68, 84, 85, 87, 88, 94, 96, 101, 107, 113, 119, 128, 135-156, 174, 175, 179
Fijian, 26
Filmore, President, 76
Finsbury Park Empire, 96
Fisher, Jerry, 92-94, 151
Folies Begere, 85
Francis I, 34
Frankland, C.H., 59
Fregoli, 99
Fun and Fancy Free, 124, 125

G

Gallanger, 194
Gastromancy, 18
Ghost, 24, 42
Golders Green Theatre, 127
Goolden, Richard, 154-155
Gospel Vents, 179
Grapevine News, 152
Great Gabbo, 106, 107, 110, 111
Greece, 18-22
Greek, 18-22
Green, James, 168
Gregory, St, 24
Griff, 105
Guest, Clifford, 170, 171, 194
Guinea, 25

H

Haliday, Bryant, 111
Hall, Terry, 166, 167, 187
Halomancy, 14
Hancock, Tony, 132, 147
Handle, G.F., 42
Harlaam, 39
Harrington, Johnathan, 60, 62
Harris, Keith, 167
Hart, Johnny, 179
Hartley, Julie, 96
Haruspicy, 14, 19
Haskey, Thomas, 55
Hebrew, 16, 17
Helen Morgan Club, 114, 116
Henry VIII, 30
Henson, Jim, 174-177
Hetch, Ben, 107
Higsby, Humphrey, 171
Hicks Hall, 47, 49
Hippocrates, 18
Hogarth, William, 46, 49
Holborn Theatre, 113
Howdy Doody, 171
Honeyman, Samuel, 41, 42
Hopkins, Anthony, 109
Hopkins, Matthew, 33, 34
Hughs, John, 42
Hydromancy, 14

I

Idol, 13
Illusion, 11, 13, 32, 120
Imitator, 60, 181
Insull, Len, 28, 29, 128, 144, 146, 147
International Brotherhood of Ventriloquists, 152
Isaiah, 16, 18, 23
Israel, 16
Israelites, 16

J

Jacobi, Barbara, 39
Jacobs, Mr., 68
Jacques, Hattie, 130, 132
James I, 34
James, Val & Fitz, 58
Jazz Singer, The 107
Jester, G.W., 75, 76
Jesus Christ, 22
Joachim, 39
Jolson, Al, 107, 116
Johnson, Jay, 178
Josephine, Empress, 53
Jugglers, 44, 51, 55

K

Kaptain Kangaroo, 171
Kennedy, Harry, 85, 181
Kermit, 175
Kimber, Bobby, 53
King, Neville, 194
King, Thomas, 42
Klinker, Effie, 122, 124

L

Lamb Chop, 170
Lambert, Walter, 102, 104-106
Lamour, Dorothy, 116
Lamouret, Robert, 172
Larynx, 180, 184
Laura, 114
Layne, Ricky, 169
LeMare, 48, 49, 86, 87, 94, 138, 140
Lemouret, Robert, 172, 173
Lenny Lion, 166, 187
Lester, Harry, 100, 101, 140, 141, 152, 182-185, 193
Letter of Introduction, 120
Le Ventriloque Ou L'Engastrimythi, 50-51
Lewis, Shari, 170
Lexiphanes, 24
Lincoln, President, 76
Lip control, 80, 188-193
Litchenstien, Prince, 49
Loggon, Thomas, 44
Lord Charles, 144, 167
Love W.E., 71, 72, 73, 75, 76, 181
Lucas, Ronn, 175
Lucian, 11, 13, 24
Luke, St., 22
Lyon, Capt. W.E., 26

M

"M" 192, 193
Maccabe, Frederic, 74, 75, 76, 139, 153, 188
Mack, Charles, 114, 140, 141
Mack, Theodore, 101, 107, 113, 140, 141
MacLeroy, James, 47
Magic, 11, 13, 14, 25, 32
Magic, 109, 143, 153
Magician, 11, 14, 24, 25, 44, 55, 58, 59, 68, 69, 99
Mahoney, Jerry, 141, 164, 171
Margaret Ann, 109
Marshall, Frank, 135, 141
Marshall, Jay, 169
Mathews, Charles, 58, 183
McCarthy, Charlie, 112-126, 130, 141, 143, 152, 175, 177, 184, 187
McElroy, George, Glenn, 142, 143
Medium, 25

Winsor, Justin, 68
Witch, 16, 17, 18, 23, 30
Witchcraft, 24, 29-37
Witchdoctor, 26
Witchfinder, 32, 33
Witchunting 29, 32
Wizards, 16, 18
Woodin, W.S., 75, 76
Wood, W.H., 152
Worsley, Arthur, 151, 168, 169
Wyman, John, 76

Y

You Can't Cheat An Honest Man, 118, 120

Z

Zulu, 26

VALENTINE VOX

Valentine Vox has been talking to himself since the age of ten and is now one of the world's masters of the ventriloquial art. The late Edgar Bergen once referred to him as 'a dishonest ventriloquist.' When asked to explain this, he said, 'He doesn't move his lips.'

For many years Valentine has delighted audiences in theatre, cabaret and on television. A veteran of the small screen, he has appeared on major networks around the world and has supported some of the biggest names in the business. He has also starred in his own network show in Britain.

Globe-trotting with his zany dog character Jorge, he has performed in nightclubs and cabaret venues from Las Vegas to Tokyo. His skill as an international artiste was perhaps summed up by one Berlin press report which said, 'Valentine Vox not only proves with ease that he is a master of his art, but remarkably he manages to perform in fluent German without losing his delightful English humor.'

Apart from his talent as a performer, he mounted the first exhibition of ventriloquism at London's Museum of Childhood and shortly after designed and established Europe's only Museum of Ventriloquism in St. Gallen, Switzerland.

KEY TO "POPULARITY"

Depicting Well-known Artistes of the Vaudeville Stage.

SIZE OF ORIGINAL, 13ft. by 5ft. 6in.

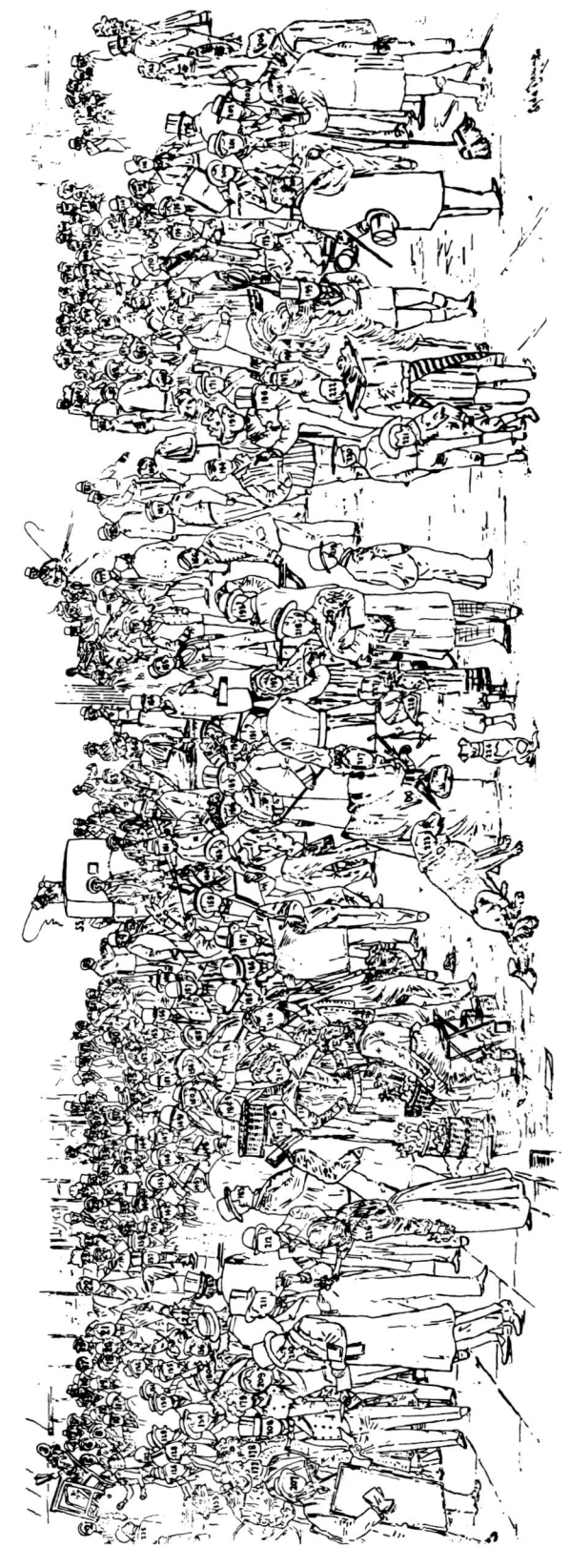

#	Name	#	Name	#	Name
1	Paul Cinquevalli	48	Harry Lauder	94	Bessie Wentworth
2	Dan Kelly	49	Paul Courtenay	95	Miss Korrie
3	Griff	50	Frank Coyne	96	Sam Glenroy
4	Allen and Hart	51	Tom Wootwall	97	Charlie Fraser
5	Tom Morris	52	Nat Clifford	98	Jeff Vendome
6	T. Morris	53	Dutch Daly	99	Mrs. Charlie Fraser
7	Harry Nation	54	Reid Pinaud	100	Grell and Grey
8	S. Ethardo	55	Chirgwin	101	Alice Maydue
9	Tom Vine	56	Walter Stockwell	102	Jerry Driscoll
10	Bros., Donaldson	57	) Two Harvey Boys	103	Bob Allinson
11		58		104	Dean Tribune
12	Wille Benn	59	Rumbo Austin	105	Jean Seul
13	Richie Tom	60	Charles Tempest	106	Ernest Rees
14	James Riley	61	Johnny Dane	107	Douglas Stuart
15	Arthur Harland	62	Arthur Pearl	108	Walter Norman
16	Albert Rollinson	63	Jack Rowley	109	Edna Cragge
17	Joe Gee (Burnells)	64	Bros. Passmore	110	Ida Heath
18	The late Pat Feeney	65		111	F. Avling
19	Jimmy Campbell	66	Bellwood Bessie	112	H. Harris
20	Albert and Edmunds	67	Harry Lester	113	) Fish and Warren
21	Pimple	68	Charlie Edwards	114	
22	Dan Leno	69	Con Fredericks	115	Jolly John Nash
23	Nellie Wilson	70	Charles Morton	116	Geo. Leybourne
24	Arthur Forrest	71	Marie Loftus	117	Will Evans
25	Nellie Richards	72	Cissie Loftus	118	May Henderson
26	John Lawson	73	Tom Branford	119	Tom Maxwell
27	Horace White	74	Charlie Clark	120	Virginia Francis
28	Tom Collins	75	Tom Costello	121	Charles Laurie
29	Lilly English	76	Clarke (Clarke and Glennie)	122	Jack Lambert
30	George Baker	77	Gus Garrick	123	Ada Lundberg
31	Fred Griffiths	78	Jock Bennett	124	Tom Holmes
32	Albert Le Fre	79	Charlie Martell	125	Kate Paradise
33	Joe Griffiths	80	Herbert Darnley	126	Wilkie Bard
34	Harry Champion	81	Geo Le Brunn	127	M'Chalk
35	Harry Anderson	82	Little Ganty	128	Charles Godfrey
36	Harry Blake (2 Bs)	83	Vene Clements	129	Jack Selbini
37	Bob Leonard	84	Carrie Laurie	130	James Norrie
38	Jack Camp	85	Marie Kendall	131	Charlie Cornish
39	Ford and Hanson	86	Daisy James	132	Fred Russell
40	Fred Millis	87	Percy Delevine	133	Florrie Ford
41	Hanson	88	Harry Delvine	134	Bransbury Williams
42	Capt. Slingsby	89	Lottie Lennox	135	J. W. Cragg
43	Tom McKay	90	Vosper	136	Alexander Dagmar
44	) Sisters Levy	91	Billie Barlow	137	Tom White
45		92	George Grey	138	Lieut. Travis
46	Mrs. Florador	93	Musical Korries	139	Cliff Ryland
47	Florador				

#	Name	#	Name
140	Barney Armstrong	186	Jack Lotto
141	Charlie Alexander	187	Wal Pink
142	Harry Randall	188	Miss Bella) Bella and Bijou
143	Herbert Campbell	189	Mr. Bijou
144	Tom O'Brien	190	Kate Carney
145	Jack Collinson	191	James Fawn
146	G. W. Hunter	192	Marie Lloyd
147	Vento	193	T. E. Dunville
148	Eddy Hanlon	194	Katie Lawrence
149	Bob Hanlon	195	Vesta Victoria
150	Teddy Bale	196	Mr. Leamy
151	George Lashwood	197	) Ara and Vora
152	Harriet Vernon	198	
153	Jenny Valmore	199	Fannie Leslie
154	Harry Gee	200	J. O'Gorman
155	Harry Pleon	201	Michael Nolan
156	Harry Freeman	202	Joe Tennyson
157	Tom Leamore	203	Horace Wheatley
158	Charles Seel	204	Walter Munroe
159	Sam Poluski	205	Johnny Dwyer
160	Ada Cerito	206	Pat Carey
161	Tom Bass	207	Harry Ford
162	Frank Folloy	208	Vesta Tilley
163	Will Poluski	209	Bessie Bonehill
164	George Mozart	210	R. G. Knowles
165	Paul Martinetti	211	Arthur Lloyd
166	Alec Hurley	212	Charles Coburn
167	Pat Raffety	213	Gus Elen
168	Arthur Lennard	214	Jenny Hill
169	Alice Lloyd	215	Peggy Pryde
170	Eugene Stratton	216	Albert Chevalier
171	George Robey	217	Arthur Rigby
172	Jimmie Hall	218	Papa Brown
173	Bill Horne	219	Little Tich
174	George Le Clercq	220	) Carrie Lorrie's Juveniles
175	Chris Horne	221	
176	Charlie Fontaine	222	Character
177	Lydia Dreams	223	Mrs. Smith's Dog
178	Jessie Preston	224	Dany George's Dog Rosie
179	Georgina Preston	225	T. Beck
180	H. Missouri	226	Artist's Wife
181	J. Sothern	227	Child of Artist
182	Will Oliver	228	Child of Artist
183	Fred McNaughton	229	Child of Artist
184	Tom McNaughton	230	Will Crackles
185	Joe Elvin	231	Jack Rich

WILL GOLDSTON Ltd.   ALADDIN HOUSE, 14 GREEN STREET, LEICESTER SQUARE, LONDON, W.C.2

PERFECT!
STRONG!!
LIFELIKE!!!

: MADE :
under the
supervision
:: :: of :: ::
Arthur Prince

No. 523.
The Soldier Boy.
£4.10.0   Carriage 1/6

No. 524. Artful Jim.
The Smoking Figure.
£8.8   Carriage 1/6

No. 525.
'Andsome 'Arry.
£4.4   Carriage 1/6

No. 526.
VENT
HEAD.
Glass eyes and
improved lip
and mouth
movement.

42/-, 60/-
and 80/-
Postage 1/-

Ventriloquial Figures for the Beginner.
Miniature Boy or Girl Doll, movable mouth, 21/-, postage 9d. Knee figure—Man, Woman, Boy or Girl. Well dressed, movable mouth and eyes. 63/- each, post paid. Superior, 90/-. Head—good expression, well constructed, 25/-, 35/-, 42/- and 50/- each. Carriage and Packing 3/-

Professional Figures.
Figure with head modelled to own design. Good glass eyes, mouth and lip movements. Smartly dressed, £6/10/0 to £25/0/0. Each of the following movements 7/6 extra:—Smoking, Winking, Arm, Leg, Ears (ears to flap). Walking, 30/- to 100/- extra. Special travelling case, 30/-.

Dialogues Written.
Full rights from £3/3/0; part rights, 21/-.

Goldston's Ventriloquial Figures and Heads are World Famous.

Heads modelled from original designs.

VENT HEAD
for Beginners, 21/-
postage 1/-

No. 525a.
Miniature
Walking
Figure.
20ins. in
height. 30/-
Postage 9d.

No. 529.
JOLLY JACK.
Modelled after ARTHUR PRINCE's famous "Jim."
£10 10s.
Carriage Paid.

No. 530.
NOSEY BUTTONS.
"A.P." movements.
Well dressed.
£8 8
Carriage Paid.

No. 527. Vent Head. With glass eyes and "A.P." movement. 63/- Carriage paid.